D0975792

"**I wish I'd had this book when I was starting out.** At every level of management and leadership, this book is an undeniable resource."

—**Peter Guber,** CEO, Mandalay Entertainment Group and author of #1 *New York Times* best-seller *Tell to Win*

"**Collaboration is easy to get wrong, undermining performance.** Ricci and Wiese—two of the world's foremost experts on collaboration—show you how to get it right and deliver great results. This book is an invaluable toolkit based on what works."

—**Morten T. Hansen,** Professor, UC Berkeley and INSEAD and author of *Collaboration*

"**We at Coca-Cola Enterprises are convinced** that the next generation of productivity and innovation will be enabled by our engaged people, well-defined communication and collaboration processes, and available technologies. Every business leader should be asking the same questions about their culture and how ready it is to compete in the 21st century."

—**Esat Sezer**, CIO, Coca-Cola Enterprises

"**Technology can shrink the globe and make every person your neighbor,** but real collaboration is still about process and culture. The combination of CVS, with local presence, and Caremark, with a total view of the patient, demonstrates the power of collaboration to create new ways to deliver health care at tremendous scale and speed. *The Collaboration Imperative* captures this holistic vision with pragmatic ways for business leaders to put collaboration to work in their organizations."

—**Stuart McGuigan**, CIO, CVS Caremark

"**In the world of services, all our activities have to be focused** on the external customer, and we must integrate and collaborate to provide the seamless service that the customer needs. Good collaboration must be well structured, and the necessary tools are no longer beyond us."

—**Adam Gade**, CIO, Maersk Line

"**Improving our ability to collaborate is extremely important** to increasing our ability to compete. *The Collaboration Imperative* gives you practical things you can do to move the needle on getting people to work better together."

—**Sheikh Mohammed Bin Essa Al Khalifa**, CEO, Bahrain Economic Development Board

THE COLLABORATION IMPERATIVE

THE COLLABORATION IMPERATIVE

→ *Executive Strategies for Unlocking Your Organization's True Potential* ←

RON RICCI CARL WIESE

Edited by Molly Davis and Ewan Morrison
Published By Cisco Systems
San Jose, California

Published 2011

Cover and Book Design by Volume Inc., San Francisco, CA.

Printed in China

ISBN 978-0-9839417-0-5

This book is dedicated to business leaders everywhere who realize that the true power of their organizations resides in their people.

CONTENTS

PART III: TECHNOLOGY

FOREWARD

The secret to success in the 21st century is not just inspiration and perspiration, but also collaboration.

In today's world, success is not driven by an individual sitting alone in a room, designing and executing an opportunity or solving a problem. The exponential complexity of forces that bear upon success require interdisciplinary skills, competencies, diversity, agility and experiences in which the whole is greater than the sum of its parts. As a result, embracing a future in which we wait for that proverbial "light at the end of the tunnel" to reveal itself so leaders in an organization can wrap their arms around it can lead to quick and unforgiving consequences. The rate of change is so ferocious that the requirement for certainty will hijack your organization's capital—both intellectual and financial.

Yet, every company has in its arsenal the resources and resourcefulness to combat and conquer these challenges, if it deploys them with a collaborative approach as Ricci and Wiese elegantly explain, exhort and encourage folks to take in *The Collaboration Imperative*. I've experienced firsthand the transformative results of the collaboration imperative in various sectors of professional business adventures.

In the entertainment business, where I've had the opportunity to build, serve and own the largest companies and the biggest films, while the journey usually begins with an individual's conceit or idea, success is always born from a vision, not a consensus. Today, this individual vision is likely the only solitary event in an involved process that can take years and cost hundreds of millions of dollars to complete—all culminating in one do-or-die Friday night opening where the tale of success or failure is told.

Despite the solitary, visionary inception, collaboration is the mantra for great cinematic endeavors. You have to outsource writers; digital technology experts for such diverse components as computer graphics, sound and special effects; actors and other performers, who are amongst the most temperamental individuals on the planet and feel they invented the cinema; filmmakers, who are at any one moment pigheaded and inspired; marketing folks who feel the film's success is solely dependent on their ability to sell it; and financial mavens who often perceive that you're shooting the budget and use that as a weapon to insert their own ideas. Let's not forget cinematographers, production designers, composers and, of course, corporate executives far removed from the bustle of the film location who can't help but constantly refer to it as "my film." The circle further widens to media, boards of directors and shareholders—all of whom are part and parcel of the collaborative journey that culminates in a hit.

It's a marvel that any film gets made, let alone realizes that initial vision. More often than not, collaboration isn't effectively maintained throughout the long journey or, in some other way, the vision gets lost. When this happens in the movie business, there's a name for it. It's called a flop, and I know what I'm talking about—I've had my share. I've learned that to avoid flops, leaders must create a culture in which consensus seeking, isolation and barriers to effective communication aren't the status quo and are instead eliminated, while collaboration, authenticity, knowledge sharing, transparency and accountability become the norm. A culture of collaboration must start at the top, but it must also be owned at the bottom.

The collaboration imperative is equally true in the ownership and management of sports franchises. Having owned professional baseball and hockey teams—and now as owner and co-executive chairman of the NBA's Golden State Warriors in the San Francisco Bay Area—I've learned that the secret sauce to success is creating and fostering a collaborative culture within the disparate team components through open communication, using technology tools to truly connect, not merely as weapons of ego. We offer incentives that provide rewards for collaborative behavior and appropriate results, and we have quick, efficient and open feedback mechanisms to create an acute sensitivity to real-time changes so we can promptly change course. This is true whether our goal is attracting elite players to make our team a perennial contender, growing a loyal audience or appealing to sponsors and advertisers. Most importantly, I've learned that successful collaboration cannot merely be deployed; it has to be embraced by every person from the owner to the laundry crew.

Success is often an arduous and uncertain journey. In sports, movies, corporate enterprises, nonprofits, governments and all other entities, there are no guarantees. It would be great to have a strategy to just make hits or just win games all the time. Failure is often an inevitable speed bump on the road to success, and every journey has a puncture or two. What's important is to have a strategy that mitigates risk and propels success, and today that means making sure everyone in your organization is liberated and incented to contribute his or her best to your collective success. *The Collaboration*

Imperative reveals this as the DNA of success. I wish I'd had this book when I was starting out. At every level of management and leadership, this book is an undeniable resource.

Collaboration is an imperative, and its call to action is to start now to realize and reap future rewards gained from discovering that within the collaborative group lies the light at the end of the tunnel.

Peter Guber
CEO, Mandalay Entertainment Group
Owner and Co-Executive Chairman,
The Golden State Warriors
Author, #1 *New York Times* Bestseller, *Tell to Win*
Los Angeles, California
September 6, 2011

INTRODUCTION

I've had the sincere privilege during my career to speak with business leaders all over the world, in companies large and small, in just about every industry. Listening to what's on their minds—what they are excited about, what keeps them up at night—is one of the most important things I do at Cisco. By listening to a wide variety of smart and passionate people, I can bring their perspectives back into Cisco which helps us improve our efforts to change the way we live, work, play and learn in new and positive ways.

As the network continues to reshape the workplace, one of the things I hear most consistently from leaders is an interest and excitement in the power of collaboration to help people within their organizations to work better together, to empower the talent of their employees and to adapt with agility to new emerging market opportunities.

The business leaders I meet with are asking us to innovate in the area of collaboration. I am committed to driving Cisco to deliver the best possible network architectures to help make successful collaboration a reality within their companies. But in hearing from companies about their collaboration journeys, and in learning from Cisco's own, it's also very clear that collaborative success does not come from technology alone, and that's what *The Collaboration Imperative* is all about.

Ron Ricci and Carl Wiese are both passionate practitioners of collaboration who've devoted much of their careers to understanding the factors involved in harnessing its potential. It comes down to this: A company's culture and processes have to evolve along with the technology. It's our sincere hope that the perspectives shared in this book will help you to achieve the greatest level of collaborative success possible and, in doing so, unlock your organization's true potential.

John T. Chambers
Chairman and CEO, Cisco
San Jose, California
September 29, 2011

1

COLLABORATION MATTERS

Why you'll embrace collaborative business practices or live to regret it.

DISCOVER THE REWARDS

CULTURE
TECHNOLOGY
PROCESS

OF COLLABORATIVE PRACTICES

EXECUTIVE SUMMARY

Improved collaboration represents your best opportunity to tap the full range of talents of your people, move with greater speed and flexibility, and compete to win over the next decade.

Building a collaborative organization requires a transformative approach to culture, processes and technology—along with an unwavering commitment from top to bottom. If you foster a culture that encourages collaborative behaviors, put processes in place to help people work better together and adopt technologies that facilitate collaboration, your efforts will be rewarded with an energized organization that can adapt quickly to changing markets and deliver results.

Across every organization lies hidden treasure just waiting to be discovered. It's not hiding in a budget spreadsheet or a warehouse full of inventory. It lies within your people—in their ideas, their experiences, their focus, their energy. The more you empower them to share their knowledge and skills, the more successful your organization will be. From ideas come innovation and new forms of productivity.

Companies are learning this lesson every day as they create new ways for employees to contribute creative solutions to business challenges, especially with the Internet redefining work boundaries. Health care professionals can better treat patients, engineers can work together more seamlessly on innovations, companies can reduce cycle times, customer-service agents can find and share expertise faster and supply-chain constituents can communicate more effectively to take advantage of new opportunities to source goods and materials. The list goes on and on, and it boils down to being more adaptable and agile in the new networked business reality.

Companies everywhere are responding to three trends that are shaping a new business landscape, making speed and flexibility the most important differentiators in just about every industry across the globe:

1. *Competition comes from anywhere and everywhere.* The barriers to entry are lower than ever, and you cannot predict who will enter your market next. It might be a startup in India, China, Africa or Eastern Europe—or competition from another industry. How do you stay ahead when you don't know which organizations you'll compete with next month or next year?
2. *Companies often have to focus on core competencies and partner to do everything else.* Where it was once an advantage to own every aspect of a value chain with the goal of vertically integrating an industry, today it makes more sense to focus on the aspect of the value chain that is most critical to your success and partner for the rest. The "core vs. context" approach is just as relevant today as when it was introduced. Narrow your focus to just what you do best, and then drive operational excellence from start to finish.
3. *Open systems change the game.* The Internet is the most disruptive force in the history of business. It's hard to remember a time before email and instant access to all kinds of information. The Internet and networking technologies connect us in ways once thought impossible, opening the door for innovative business models. Think about e-commerce, online financial services, and supply chain and sales force automation. But now, businesses must adapt to another wave of networked technology that is shaping the modern working experience into one that is mobile, social, virtual and driven by video communications.

What do these trends mean for business leaders? Together, they create an urgent need for increased adaptability. In this environment, the most important step you can take to maximize future success is to build flexibility into your business practices and increase the speed with which you can adjust your strategy to capitalize on fast-moving market transitions.

EXPERT TIP ON ADAPTING

"If your organization cannot adapt, evolve and respond to the expectations and desires of the people you're serving—including your employees—you will fall in their estimation and find your company mired in mediocrity."

—Professor Tony O'Driscoll, Duke University Fuqua School of Business

The technology that runs our companies and our lives is fast, open, decentralized and highly adaptable. What if organizations followed the same model? How would that change the way we work, and what benefits could emerge from the transformation? This book explores the answers to these questions.

Just as the initial emergence of the Internet changed everything, we're now in the early stages of another fundamental shift. It's the decade of collaboration—a time when people who've never met find each other and work together, and employees at any level or any remote corner of an organization can provide the spark for your next important innovation. Collaboration is your best opportunity for building an enterprise that can adapt to fast-changing market pressures. It helps you achieve operational excellence today and deliver innovation tomorrow.

Imagine an organization in which people:

- → Communicate openly across business functions and departments
- → Are always aware of the company's objectives and priorities, even as they rapidly evolve
- → Perform multiple different roles during the day
- → Self-select for projects based on interest, expertise and importance to the business
- → Locate needed information in real time
- → Work as mobile and distributed participants—even beyond the walls of the company—as partners, customers, contractors and suppliers

When you allow people to collaborate well, the organization captures value you simply cannot discover through a more rigid approach. If Six Sigma, the management philosophy originated by Motorola and popularized by General Electric, Honeywell and others, is about driving variation out of your processes, one of the benefits of collaboration is its ability to bring more variation in.[1] This means tapping into a larger, more diverse pool of people. Some of these people will report to you, others will not. Some will come from partners, suppliers or other organizations within your business ecosystem, including your customers or competitors.

The benefits of this increased diversity run deep. For example, you can:

- → Empower people to contribute important ideas and experiences
- → Shorten product development or sales cycle times
- → Increase employee productivity

Collaboration is about maximizing the value inherent in the diversity of your people.

- → Align teams around your organization's larger shared goals
- → Move quickly from strategy to execution
- → Identify and eradicate organizational overlaps
- → Ensure knowledge and resources sharing
- → Spark product and business model innovation
- → Save money across the organization

But We're Already Collaborating, Aren't We?

Every time you send a group email, convene a cross-functional meeting, host a Web conference, post a comment on a discussion forum or contribute to a company wiki, you're collaborating. But this is the proverbial tip of the iceberg.

Solving the CEO's Conundrum

With few exceptions, every successful organization faces the same challenge: How do we operate at peak performance today while also setting ourselves up for success tomorrow?

We call this the CEO's Conundrum. And it doesn't matter if you're a Fortune 500 company or a garage-based startup of savvy entrepreneurs, the challenge remains the same.

Collaboration allows you to bring together the right people at the right time to make the most informed decisions. It enables you to address fast-moving opportunities and helps you balance operational excellence and innovation in a way that solves the CEO's Conundrum.

Collaboration is much more than communications. It is the way that people in an organization function together. Better collaboration means better business operations and, ultimately, better results—faster.

Most companies today collaborate vertically (with

suppliers and distributors, for example), but future collaboration will increasingly extend to broader "flash" communities—small groups of specialized players that might include cross-functional teams, customers, partners, universities, even competitors. As people learn to collaborate better, you'll see nimble teams of subject-matter experts form quickly to get work done and then disband just as fast, only to reconfigure again to focus on the next problem or opportunity.

These smaller, nimbler teams drive results by drawing experts to projects rather than assigning them top-down. With effective collaboration, your people are empowered by new organizational cultures that celebrate a diversity of talents and promote not only the sharing of knowledge and resources, but also of accountability and rewards.

Let's be clear—collaboration is not about achieving consensus. In fact, consensus is the enemy of collaboration. For collaboration to unlock your people's best work, you'll need to create the conditions for collaboration to flourish. Channel the diversity of your people by creating processes that allow your company to reap the benefits of more perspectives while making it clear who has decision-making rights. Set the expectation that once decisions are made, collaborative efforts move from exploring and debating possibilities to executing outcomes. Pervasive collaboration technologies connect these teams. The technology toolbox is constantly evolving to help teams align and mobilize across geographies, time zones and organizational boundaries.

Consensus is the enemy of collaboration.

You are collaborating, but there is more to explore. All around us, companies are embracing collaborative behavior. It's up to business leaders like you to chart a course for collaboration that works for your organization. Here's the challenge: It's harder than you might expect to get the job done right.

Q&A

The Future of Work Has Arrived

Here, Dr. Thomas W. Malone, the Patrick J. McGovern Professor of Management at the MIT Sloan School of Management and Founding Director of the MIT Center for Collective Intelligence, as well as the author of the seminal book *The Future of Work,* discusses how the intersection of technology innovation and work practices is driving collaboration.

Q: How is increased decentralization and networked collaboration changing the nature of work?

A: We're now in the early stages of an increase in human freedom in business that—in the long run—may be as important for business as the change to democracies was for governments. It's now possible for the first time in human history to have the economic benefits of large organizations and the human benefits of very small organizations—flexibility, creativity, motivation and freedom.

This is possible now because a new generation of information technologies is reducing the cost of communication and information sharing to very low levels. This makes it possible for huge numbers of people, even in large organizations, to have enough information to make sensible decisions on their own instead of waiting for orders from someone above them who supposedly knows more than they do.

Q: What are the benefits of the proliferation of low-cost communication and information sharing?

A: A bunch of nice things happen when people make decisions for themselves instead of just following orders. They often are much more highly motivated. They're willing to work harder. They're more creative. Decision empowerment lets people be more flexible and adaptable, which can allow them to serve customers better. Even though it won't happen everywhere, this shift toward increased decentralized decision making, toward more human freedom in business, is likely to happen in more areas of our economy over the coming decades.

Q: Is decentralization always a good thing?

A: I certainly don't believe that everything should be decentralized all the time. There's obviously a trade off. Part of what managers need to do in this new world is to sharpen their ability to know when a centralized or a decentralized approach is best. Loosely speaking, you should decentralize things only when the benefits of doing so are greater than the costs or the risks.

If your organization is imaginative, you can often design new decentralized ways of doing things that let you reap the advantages of decentralization while avoiding many of the usual risks. In other words, you can find ways to establish hard and fast parameters that provide the necessary structure to minimize the risks associated with more collaborative business practices but still give you the ability to benefit from a more participative, inclusive, dynamic approach.

Q: Can you define "collective intelligence" and explain its significance to business leaders?

A: Collective intelligence can be defined as groups of individuals acting collectively in ways that seem intelligent. By that definition, collective intelligence has existed at least as long as there have been people. Families, countries, companies and armies are all examples of groups of people working together in ways that, at least sometimes, seem intelligent. What is new, however, is that in the last few years we've seen some very new kinds of collective intelligence enabled by the Internet, and I think we are still in the early stages of leveraging these new kinds of collective intelligence in business.

In the 20th century, much of business involved relatively routine industrial processes. In the 21st century, the critical factors in business success often involve how rapidly a company can innovate, how quickly it can respond to changing situations. In other words, the success of a company increasingly depends not just on how efficient it is, but on how intelligent it is. So I think the phrase *collective intelligence* helps us direct our attention to some of the issues that are especially important in our increasingly knowledge-based economy.

Q: What does this mean for executive management styles?

A: They need to move from the traditional view of management as command and control to a much more flexible view of management, one I call *coordinate and cultivate.* By coordinate and cultivate, I don't mean the opposites of command and control. I mean the whole spectrum of possibilities from top down, centralized, command and control on one end, to bottom up, decentralized, facilitation on the other end. People who are good at coordinating and cultivating are good at adapting what they do to the situations in which they find themselves, and moving very flexibly all along that spectrum, from top down to bottom up, as the situation demands.

Q: What are some of the key considerations for success with coordination and cultivation?

A: There are two great paradoxes that every executive has to appreciate and learn. The first paradox is what I call the *paradox of standards,* which says that sometimes rigid standards can enable more flexibility and decentralization in other parts of the same system.

A prime example of that is the Internet itself. The Internet Protocol, or IP, is a rigid standard for how people exchange information over the Internet. It's exactly the same everywhere in the world. In part, it's precisely because that standard is so rigid that all the other flexibility and decentralization we associate with the Internet is possible.

In the case of businesses, what we need are standards, perhaps things like product-quality standards, or service-level agreements or financial-reporting standards. If you can pick the right standards at the right places, then you can often leave people much more freedom to do many more things at other levels as long as they meet those standards at the key places you specified. That's the paradox of standards.

> The other paradox is what I call the *paradox of power,* which says that sometimes the best way to gain power is to give it away. For instance, Pierre Omidyar, the founder of eBay, gave power away to customers. Linus Torvalds, the leader of the Linux open source software community, gave power away to programmers all over the world. But in each case, these leaders were rewarded with a different kind of power. That's the paradox of power.

The Challenge of Collaboration

Conventional wisdom holds that a willingness to work together toward a common goal can make collaboration work. In most cases, this is not enough.

Collaboration is not easy. Collaborative teams are increasingly virtual, dispersed or cross-functional, and composed of members who may never have met each other before. Perhaps they come from different social or cultural backgrounds. They might come from dysfunctional organizations (and you certainly don't want them to bring their bad habits with them), or for a variety of reasons they may not be fully committed to the team's work or feel accountable for its success. Not surprisingly, it's even harder to build good chemistry in this new world of virtual teaming.

Given these challenges, collaboration should not be delivered piecemeal or just be a poster on a wall; it cannot be introduced with fanfare only to be relegated to the dustbin of good ideas because of a lack of sustained commitment. There are things that you can do to improve collaboration immediately, and there are more transformative steps you can take to build a more collaborative organization in the future.

To evolve more collaborative organizational capabilities, you will have to cultivate and coordinate three components of collaboration: *culture, process* and *technology.* To that end, the three main sections of this book are dedicated to these topics. It's a trifecta of change (which is why you can't depend on *just* your IT organization to lead the effort). Your collaboration-building effort needs to be led by a collaborative team that includes leadership from top management, human resources, marketing and sales, operations, back office, research and development, customer service or other key functions, as well as representatives from different levels of the organization, to provide authentic employee perspectives.

Culture, process, technology: Let's take a quick look at each one.

COLLABORATION SUCCESS

Culture

An organization's culture refers to the people within it and the norms by which they operate. It's about how they treat each other and how they interact and communicate. Companies that collaborate well share cultural similarities. Employees trust each other and share information readily to best serve the needs of the overall business. They communicate often and openly. They know how to tap specialized knowledge in other parts of the organization.

And they are eager to partner with each other and with others outside of the company.

Collaboration can't simply be *deployed*; it needs to be ***embraced***. And for that, you need your people on board and committed. We can't state explicitly enough that this includes your leaders. Executive buy-in and participation is imperative. Executives must be willing participants—modeling collaborative behavior and embracing the technology tools—not just taskmasters.

In our section on culture, we talk about how collaborative leaders can model behaviors that others in the organization will follow. We discuss how to foster a culture that encourages your people to embrace your organization's most important priorities and business objectives as the shared goals everyone works together to achieve. Then we explore the important role of authentic communication in collaboration by leading you through a self assessment to discover your own communication style. You'll also learn how to recognize the communication preferences of others, as well as best practices for communicating with the increasingly diverse and virtual teams on which we all participate today.

As a culture of collaboration takes hold, it mitigates a common operational barrier for many companies—internal competition between departmental, functional or geographical teams for human and financial resources. When internal competition escalates, so do passive-aggressive behaviors as teams fight for the same limited share of resources and credit. It promotes knowledge hoarding and needless redundancy that drains corporate resources, distracts workers and keeps companies from moving quickly. Collaboration does just the opposite. It exposes the overlaps in your organization and moves your company from a culture of internal competition to a culture of shared goals. This becomes the platform for achieving business results faster.

Process

Processes reflect the way we get work done. When it comes to collaboration, the most important processes are those that involve interactions between people. Think of collaborative processes as the institutional support structures necessary for helping people implement the strategy.

Companies that are good at collaboration understand that traditional systems of performance do not work as well in the new business landscape. It's hard to promote collaboration, for example, when the company recognizes and rewards workers strictly on individual or departmental achievements.

> Collaboration is not about automating the present; it's about optimizing the future.

Your company must retool management models and human resources to promote collaborative efforts and achievements. To maximize collaborative success, it's essential to provide incentives for the people within your organization to change engrained behaviors. It's not enough to automate the present; you need to optimize for the future.

There is no cookie-cutter approach to developing collaborative processes. All organizations—even ones in the same industry—are unique. Each one needs to assess its distinct business processes to determine where increased collaboration can drive improvement. In this section of the book, we share three examples of processes that help leaders and employees work better together. Learning more about these processes will also help you to begin looking at other areas of your business where people interact that may also benefit from a more collaborative approach.

First, we begin with a process to establish a common vocabulary for communicating both the decisions an organization makes and the shared goals that result from those decisions. We believe this concept of a common vocabulary is crucial for collaboration success. Establishing a common vocabulary fuels transparent decision making, minimizes second-guessing and creates faster alignment and commitment to the shared goals your people will strive to achieve. Second, we share a process to help collaborative teams create trust quickly, enabling them to understand their purpose, define individual roles and accountability, and clarify what leaders expect the team to achieve. Lastly, we share a process to help teams get more value out of the meetings they attend and provide some tips on conducting effective virtual meetings.

Technology

In the networked world, collaboration technologies connect distributed, global teams. A decade ago, the first wave of Internet-enabled tools focused on personal productivity and technology convergence that formed a base for the pervasive, networked collaboration that's taking place today. Now we see an emphasis on process productivity and wider engagement across departments and business functions, as mobile, social, virtual and video technologies help teams collaborate to adapt more quickly to market transitions.

The most successful collaboration initiatives address real business needs.

The pace of innovation for collaboration technologies is remarkable and will only result in better tools for workers as time goes on. When considering these technologies, it's important to lead with business objectives and focus on the mix of collaboration tools that best helps your organization meet those goals. It's equally important to resist the temptation to acquire the latest technology before you define a collaboration strategy.

In the technology section of this book, we examine how

the portfolio of collaboration tools—including unified Internet Protocol (IP) Communications, mobile applications, video and telepresence, conferencing, messaging, enterprise social software and customer care solutions—empower the people in an organization. Next, we highlight eight opportunities for collaboration technologies to make a major impact on your business. Lastly, we explore the return on investment of collaboration technologies in operational, productivity and strategic terms. Is collaboration worth it? You be the judge.

Many Questions, One Answer: Collaboration

- → How can we ensure that our employees make the best use of the information available?
- → How can we manage operational and capital costs in the face of increasing needs from the business?
- → How can we reduce expenses but maintain deep customer relationships?
- → How can we build trust with colleagues, customers and partners when we can't be in front of them as frequently?
- → How can we improve service when we have so many more customers to reach?

Why We Wrote This Book

Over the past several years, we've spent thousands of hours on the subject of collaboration. We've met with customers and partners from around the world. We've engaged with academic thought leaders and researchers from leading universities. We've exchanged ideas and best practices with C-level executives from all kinds of industries and from large and small enterprises. We spend the majority of our days studying how to maximize the power of collaboration in this hyper-connected world. Above all, our customers told us this effort was important.

We wrote this book to help business leaders improve collaboration and enhance their overall performance. The book offers practical tips and strategies for making your company more collaborative today and in the future. We avoid Ivory Tower theory and business-speak in favor of useful ideas, tools, strategies and case studies from a variety of entities—each on its own collaboration journey.

Here are some of the surprising facts and hands-on advice contained in the following pages:

→ The biggest barriers to collaboration are not technical. They are cultural and organizational in nature.
→ Collaboration cannot be deployed—it must be embraced.
→ Consensus can be the enemy of collaboration.
→ Good ideas can come from anywhere, and the more voices you have, the better.
→ Collaboration success means changing both roles and rewards.
→ "Knowledge accidents" are a good thing.
→ Companies that enable employees to interact more create more value.
→ Collaboration requires stronger personal communications skills.
→ Although collaboration is about decentralizing, it has to start at the top.
→ If collaboration isn't producing demonstrable results, chances are that your culture is resistant or that technology deployments are not properly aligned with your organization's processes.
→ You get out of collaboration what you put in.
→ The average return on collaboration is four times a company's initial investment.

1 2 3 4 5 6 7 8 9 10

We hope this book will be the catalyst for important and lasting change in your company and will serve as a valuable resource that you'll return to again and again.

The Way Forward

To affect real change, you'll have to integrate a collaborative culture with collaborative processes and technologies into a tailor-made strategy for your organization. Failure to make sufficient changes in one area will likely hamper your efforts overall.

Collaboration is not a turn-key proposition. Success requires a sustained commitment to transforming your organization's culture, processes and technology. When approached in this way, collaboration represents the single most important investment you can make. It will drive the next wave of business growth, innovation and productivity. It will help you capture the biggest opportunities and tackle the most challenging issues over the next decade by empowering your people to contribute the diversity of their ideas and energy. This ignites their passion around a common purpose and inspires them to move with agility to achieve success together.

If you are not yet embracing a collaborative future, your competitors may already have an edge. Don't get left behind. Systemic transformation is something that each organization needs to address on its own. It's about assessing your business objectives and needs as well as your assets, strengths and weaknesses to institute the changes that work best for you. Use this book as a guide to creating the conditions that allow collaboration to flourish.

60 SECOND WRAP

:00	The rapidly changing global business environment is compelling organizations to become more adaptable.
:15	Collaboration strategies can help companies meet this challenge by balancing operational excellence with innovation.
:20	Businesses that collaborate better will realize their full potential and sustain a competitive advantage.
:25	Collaboration success depends on three critical components: culture, process and technology.
:30	Replace internal competition with a culture of shared goals, and encourage sharing and other collaborative behaviors.
:35	Put collaborative processes in place, such as a common vocabulary and team charter, to help people work better together.
:40	Assemble a portfolio of integrated technologies that facilitates collaboration.
:50	Assess your business objectives as well as your assets, strengths and weaknesses to institute the changes that work best for you.
:55	Many leading organizations already have mapped a course to a collaborative future. Don't get left behind.

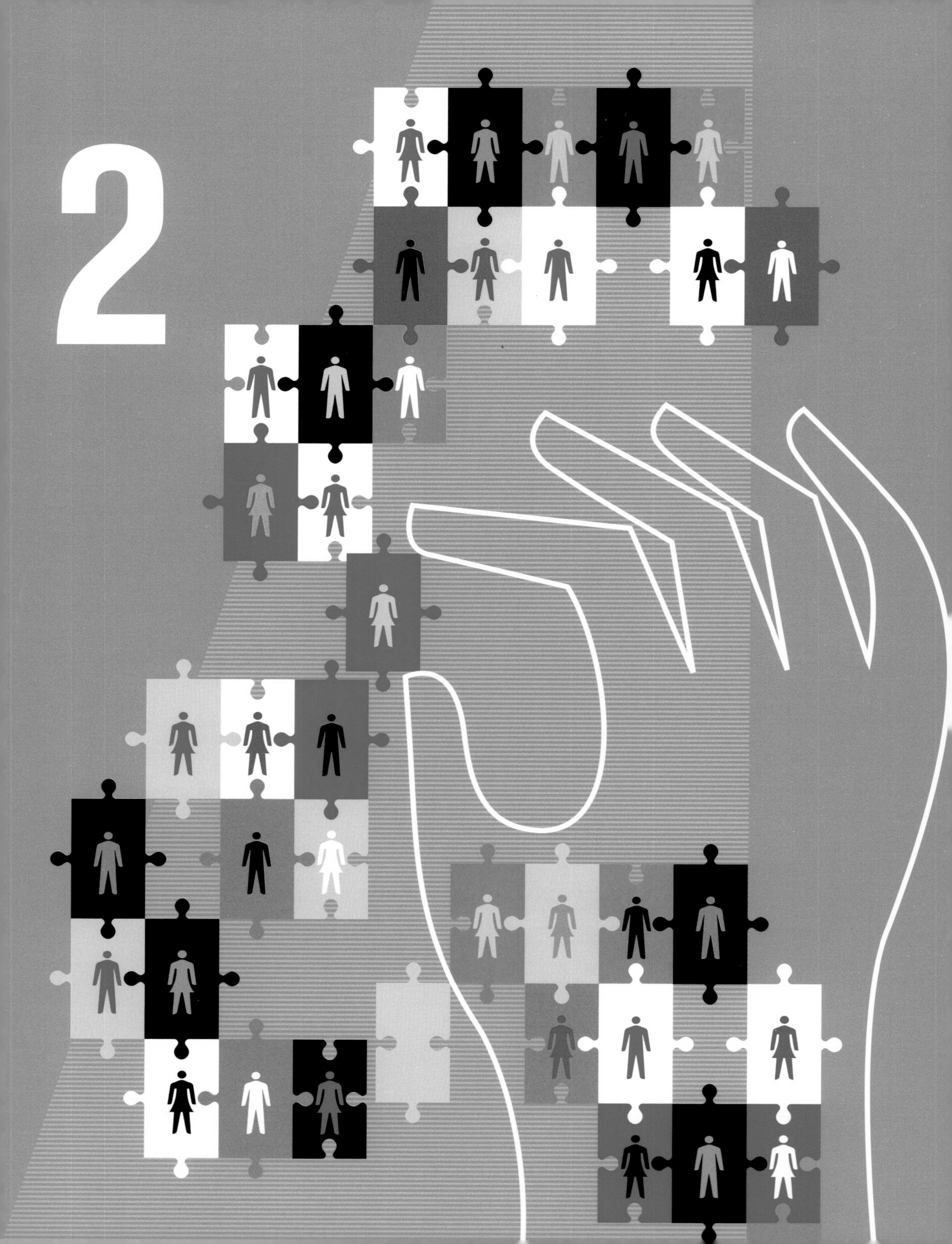

2

A COLLABORATIVE CULTURE STARTS AT THE TOP

Become a chief catalyst of collaboration to create a culture of shared goals.

COLLABORATION

=

[GREATER]

1

SPEED

2

FLEXIBILITY

3

COMPETITIVENESS

EXECUTIVE SUMMARY

Collaboration transforms your organization from rigid to flexible, from slow to quick. A collaborative culture emphasizes shared goals. It drives the right behaviors in your people when you approach decision making with transparency in mind and reward them for sharing what they know.

It's been said many times that "Culture eats strategy for breakfast," and it's true; you can't delegate culture. Your behavior as a leader will be modeled by others. Never change who you are, but know what behaviors are expected of a collaborative leader if you're asking your teams to work more effectively together.

Culture derives from a written or unwritten code that represents the way that you, as a leader, want your employees to interact among themselves and with your customers, partners and the general public. It is an intangible framework that runs parallel to the visible infrastructure of an organization. And it is equally powerful in its ability to support your goals or to thwart them.

So how does a culture of teamwork and collaboration translate into speed, adaptability, productivity and innovation? We all know the challenges of organizational silos and the incentives that encourage myopic thinking. And as business leaders, we've all experienced some form of passive-aggressive behavior from our peers. We may have even slipped up ourselves every once in a while. It's not our intention to delve into deep analysis on these issues, as they are already well documented and, frankly, most of us as managers are familiar with them in one way or another. However, we all know their painful effect on team or organizational performance.

When departments work on isolated activities, they tend to protect their information and assets and compete with other departments for opportunities and resources. Knowledge gets trapped in pockets that others in the company could benefit from but cannot reach. Budget gets wasted. All the while, markets move and new opportunities emerge.

All of these issues are rooted in human behavior—either encouraged or tolerated. A culture of shared goals minimizes hoarding and competition by creating a collaborative environment that your people can experience through their work, either locally or virtually.

It's hard work. But what if the only way to compete is to reallocate budget or people—your brightest innovators and problem-solvers—to an emerging, high-impact opportunity? What if those resources and that expertise could seamlessly move to wherever they were needed next to support your shared goals? What if you could form and re-form teams easily, coordinate and make connections among those teams smoothly, and encourage leaders to act as vertical and horizontal conduits in the organization?

Collaborative cultures share information, diagnose problems, raise concerns, coordinate efforts and identify possible initiatives and transition points. It's a big promise, no doubt, but that's why it can be a game-changer.

1 2 3 4 5 6 7 8 9 10

Q&A

Imagination and Courage Fuel Successful Collaboration at General Electric

Greg Simpson, Chief Technology Officer at General Electric (GE), shares his insights about the collaborative transformation underway inside one of the world's most respected and innovative companies.

Q: How important is collaboration to GE's success, and how do you see collaboration evolving over the next decade?

A: At GE, we believe that two heads are better than one, and 300,000 are *much* better than one. But it's even bigger than that—what about the rest of the world? We want to go out to the world to get ideas, solve problems and raise our game. The more people you involve, the more ideas you get. The biggest potential for collaboration lies in the middle of the organization, but the opportunity only grows as you expand your reach, even outside your organizational walls.

Moving forward, we see collaboration becoming much more intuitive and integrated—it can't be hard. There are many ways to collaborate—from web and video conferencing to mobile devices and social media. We need to bring these pieces together more seamlessly so we can take advantage of the right tool for the right interaction.

Q: In your experience, does collaboration require culture and process transformation as well as collaborative technologies?

A: Collaboration has to be a holistic effort that includes people and processes, as well as technology. If it's just about technology, it won't work. At GE, there are a few behaviors that we expect of our employees. These include imagination, or the ability to generate new and innovative ideas, and courage, or the willingness to take risks and push ideas through the organization. It's no surprise that changing the way we work to be more collaborative reflects our culture.

GE is also very process-focused and our efforts in collaboration are no exception. Process ensures repeatability and sustainable advantage. Without process, you won't get the best out of your people or your tools. Best practices can be lost over time because they are not embedded. Things need to be simple, repeatable and scalable. Culture, process and technology are interlaced by definition. You work them independently, but you must tie them together for success.

Q: Can you give any examples of the collaborative evolution underway at GE?

A: One obvious recent change is the move toward more virtual interactions.

People are used to face-to-face communication. They have a circle of people near them who influence their ideas. What if you expand your circle beyond the people who are between you and the water cooler? What if you could stick your head into the offices of many more people in a virtual fashion? Collaboration in the digital age brings ideas together faster, and we want our people to think more broadly about whom they work with in order to get things done.

Initially, financial pressures during the economic downturn forced us to experiment with collaboration. We had to cut expenses like travel, so people were willing to try alternatives. Then we noticed that new technologies actually changed how we work—for the better.

For example, when we embraced video, we saw higher engagement in meetings. It's common for people to multitask during audio-only calls, but video changed that. When you can see me on video, I can't multitask. I pay closer attention. In another example, I can interact with people on a blog in different time zones. It's okay that it's asynchronous—it gets the conversation going. Face-to-face is still important, but you can't be everywhere. Integrating these tools makes you more effective. By having the courage to try new ways of working, you discover how effective collaboration can be, and you begin to imagine what else is possible.

Q: What advice do you have for business leaders focused on improving collaboration?

A: It's critical to lead by example. If leaders hoard information, their people will do the same thing. If a leader is open and transparent with information, his or her people will be too. Leaders must demonstrate the power of collaboration themselves if they want others to follow.

People are often afraid to adopt new behaviors unless leaders adopt them too. There was a time when email wasn't an accepted form of communication. People printed emails out, hand wrote a reply and sent them out in an inter-office envelope. But when leaders started using email to communicate, or using electronic calendars to schedule meetings, cultural acceptance followed. If you missed a meeting because you weren't using the tools, you got with the program in a hurry.

You have to be willing to experiment and try new things. Different businesses have different criteria and needs, but there are all kinds of great ideas out there. One thing is for sure: You will lose your competitive edge if you can't bring people together and harness their ideas. Without a collaboration strategy, you can't harness those ideas across the organization. Businesses are getting better and better at collaborating, and the ones that are successful will get ahead and be more competitive.

Behaviors of Collaborative Leaders

In order to become a chief catalyst for collaboration, you will have to model behaviors that embody the way you'd like your employees to work. For 150 years, corporations, governments and militaries were built for up-and-down leadership, with incentives and rewards that discouraged cross-organization thinking and, in many cases, actually created or encouraged internal competition. Your challenge is to develop and model the behaviors required to inspire people and teams to genuinely break through organizational silos and make collaboration a competitive advantage.

How you lead your people has a direct impact on your ability to eliminate or mitigate the types of human behaviors that slow organizations down. In our experience, both inside Cisco and with our customers, highly collaborative leaders share four leadership traits. They:

→ **Focus on authentic leadership and eschew passive aggressiveness**

→ **Relentlessly pursue transparent decision making**

→ **View resources as instruments of action, not as possessions**

→ **Codify the relationship between decision rights, accountability and rewards**

Focus on authentic leadership and eschew passive aggressiveness. For collaboration to succeed, leaders need to be authentic. Cisco studied which characteristics of leaders on collaborative teams are most important, and we found that the most critical attribute was a leader's willingness to follow through on commitments. This involves two elements.

First, as a leader of a team, department or business unit with people, budgets and resources under your control, you must follow through on organizational commitments. Unfortunately, people don't always do what they promise. Passive aggressiveness is a subtle, nuanced form of human behavior in which people find ways to undermine others. They often give tacit agreement in a meeting, for example, but then proceed to take counterproductive action once the meeting is over. Or they might agree to help another team, but then are slow to follow through or put an under-performer on the assignment. Think of how much organizational inertia is created because leaders don't always do what they say they will do.

EXPERT TIP ON PERSEVERANCE

> **"Leaders need resolve, resilience and determination to affect collaborative transformation. They need to 'walk the talk' for a sustained period of time."**

—Professor Tony O'Driscoll, Duke University Fuqua School of Business

Second, when there is disagreement about a decision—one made by you or someone else—fight the instinct to make it personal. Ultimately, most disagreements are not personal in nature, but rather result from differing approaches to making a decision. The more you focus on communicating what drives your decision making, the more time you can spend making good decisions instead of arguing a choice with a peer. This leads us to the next leadership trait.

Relentlessly pursue transparent decision making. Decisions are always about making choices; it's critical that you are clear about how you make them. Tell people your style and thought process for navigating tricky, or even every day, decisions. In our experience, and this is backed up by research, there's a direct relationship between the agility and resilience of a team and the transparency of its decision-making processes. When you're open and transparent about the answers to three questions—who made the decision, who is accountable for the outcomes of the decision, and is that accountability real—people in organizations spend far less time questioning how or why a decision was made. Think of how much time is wasted ferreting out details when a decision is made and communicated because the people who are affected don't know who made the decision or who is accountable for its consequences.

Answer Three Questions to Foster Transparent Decision Making

Transparent decision making requires that all stakeholders know the answers to these questions:

- → Who is making the decision?
- → Who is accountable for the outcomes of the decision?
- → What are the consequences—positive or negative—of that accountability?

In a later chapter, we discuss the importance of establishing a common vocabulary for decision making, especially as a communications platform that can scale an organization's collaborative processes. As a leader, your responsibility is to document the key decision paths of your organization and communicate them to your team as often as you can. There was a time in business when hoarding information was a source of organizational power. Today, the inverse is true if you want to motivate a team that is increasingly mobile, global and socially driven.

Explain the guiding principles of your decision-making style at each stage of your organization's decision paths. Share your biases and tell war stories of how your successes and failures shaped these biases. We often hear the phrase "intelligent risk taking"—nothing empowers people to take good risks more than understanding the conditions for taking the risk in the first place. Transparent decision making is critical to empowering your people.

View resources as instruments of action, not as possessions. The promise of flexibility and agility as an organization, inspired by establishing shared goals across organizational boundaries, is only attainable if you back it up by sharing resources as well.

Resources are not possessions of individual leaders, but instruments of action to be used in pursuit of the company's shared goals.

It's hardly a new observation that people sometimes stockpile resources around their business unit or department, or are slow—perhaps even hesitant—to share those resources with other departments. There might even be incentives in place that discourage sharing. For as long as companies have pursued profits, the size of one's organization has defined the size of one's financial opportunity. But are your resources truly applied as optimally as possible to your market opportunities in a way that best serves the total business? By unlocking these trapped resources, organizations can more quickly and successfully pursue emerging market opportunities.

Having a common approach to assess and communicate resource decisions is critical to creating a transparent environment among leaders. The more transparent the environment, the more willing leaders will be to share resources in support of the shared goals of the entire business, and the harder it will be for resisters to hoard them. This shift in approach is not an easy one for leaders to make and requires a balancing act between clear expectations, patience and follow through. Ultimately, it's as much a mindset as it is a process. The fundamental enablers of collaborative leadership are viewing resources as instruments of action rather than as possessions and aligning your company's larger shared goals to an accountability system that includes rewards and incentives for working together effectively.

Codify the relationship between decision rights, accountability and rewards. Modeling the desired collaborative behaviors—showing your employees that you walk the talk—is the goal. But what happens when you're not around? The more these behaviors are codified into an end-to-end system across your organization, the greater the odds of collaboration succeeding when you're not there to reinforce cultural norms. As you define the decision paths of your organization and build a common vocabulary to make those decision paths as transparent as possible, take the time to establish clear parameters. Who gets to make decisions? Are all decisions tied to funding? These are the types of questions to which everyone must know the answers. Publish the parameters for these decision rights and tell people which leaders have these rights—that information is crucial to breaking through any consensus logjam; decision-rights holders should have 51 percent of the vote when collaborative teams can't reach natural agreement.

Having published decision rights is just one element of an accountability system. While it's never pleasant to talk about the consequences of poor decisions, the reality is that to succeed, collaboration demands more distributed and empowered actions across your organization. With that empowerment comes not only more good outcomes but also the increased potential for bad ones. You will need to consider new ways of gaining input from teams on the quality of collaborative decision making and reward people who consistently make good decisions in a collaborative environment.

As part of their overall performance management, every Cisco employee is measured by peers and their managers on their collaboration factor, the result of which directly impacts how their performance is rated and, ultimately, the size of their total compensation. Other factors that determine the size of bonuses are tied to how well employees collectively perform in achieving certain shared goals that Cisco establishes annually, such as customer-satisfaction metrics and financial results. Collaborative cultures not only foster teamwork, they also reward it. Performance measures must strike a balance between how well employees carry out their individual roles and how much they contribute to collective outcomes.

Legendary Duke University basketball coach Mike Krzyzewski knows a thing or two about working together to reach shared goals. He reminds team members—and business leaders—that the name on the front of the jersey is more important than the name on the back of the jersey.

Q&A

Achieving Results Through Disciplined Collaboration

Sometimes collaboration produces results far greater than you could have imagined. But in many situations, collaboration simply doesn't make business sense. Here, Dr. Morten T. Hansen, a professor at the University of California at Berkeley and INSEAD, and the author of *Collaboration: How Leaders Avoid the Traps, Create Unity and Reap Big Results*, discusses the importance of exercising "disciplined collaboration."

Q: Why has collaboration become such an important part of the executive agenda?

A: A number of trends are converging to make collaboration important. First, with globalization you now have talent scattered throughout the world. So you need collaboration to successfully integrate that talent across geographies.

Second, there's been a 30-year trend of increasing fragmentation or specialization of work. You need collaboration to coordinate across those areas of specialization.

And finally, businesses have come to be organized into autonomous, or semi-autonomous, business units. So far, it's worked because these units are empowered; you can measure their results, and one person is in charge. But now we're pushing the limits of how much you can reap from this model. Companies know they're leaving additional value on the table because they're getting a lot of value from each of the units but very little value by working *across* these units. They want the synergies that are only possible through increased collaboration across the organization.

Q: Is that what "disciplined collaboration" is all about?

A: Yes, the key objective of disciplined collaboration is to extract the benefit of collaborative synergy and the decentralized model. The idea is that you focus on the business case first and collaboration second.

You must commit to driving results and recognize that collaboration is a means to an end—not an end in and of itself. This sometimes gets confused in organizations because a norm takes hold that people should be collaborating. But the reality is that your role is to create value. Sometimes that requires collaboration, and sometimes not.

So it's important as leaders to say yes to collaboration when it makes sense and to have the discipline to say no when it doesn't. When it comes to the business case for collaboration, I use the "ICE" model. The "I" is for innovation. Are there ways you can increase innovation by working across the organization? Next, look at customer interaction to see if there are ways to coordinate activities that will result in higher customer satisfaction and cross-sell. That's the "C." The "E" is for efficiency, which is achieved by sharing best practices and helping each other improve efficiency across the organization. Using this model, or another that serves the same purpose, you can establish whether there's a business case for collaboration with any project.

Q: Assuming there's a business case for collaboration, what common barriers do leaders face when pursuing a collaborative approach?

A: We see four barriers to collaboration occurring over and over. The first two are related to motivation. First we see the *not invented here* barrier. That's when people are just not willing to seek input from others outside of their own respective units.

The second barrier is *hoarding*. We've all experienced workers who may not want to provide information or help when asked. The hoarding mentality is found and often encouraged in siloed, hierarchical organizations. It's the way a lot of business leaders have been conditioned to succeed. "Knowledge is power, and I've got the knowledge, so I'm going to keep it and use it for my business unit alone."

The next two barriers are capability barriers. A *search* barrier occurs when people are not able to find the information and people that they need to collaborate effectively. They want to collaborate; they just don't know how. And this happens all the time in large companies.

The final barrier occurs when workers are not able to transfer complicated knowledge from one unit to another, what we call the *transfer* barrier. "I have this great body of information, but how do I get it to the people in Unit B?" They can't, because the technology or processes are not in place to allow for the regular exchange of information.

There are two important points about these four barriers. First, different situations have different barriers. It could be a mix. Second, you need to use the right management intervention for the right barrier. If you have a hoarding barrier and it's cultural, you need to try to change the incentive system, the culture or the norms. Information technology tools are probably not going to be as useful here. It's dangerous to go into an organization that is not set up to collaborate and simply implement technology because you haven't really addressed the key problem of, say, hoarding. So you need a multifaceted intervention. You need to look at the incentive system. You need to look at the policies, the culture and the technology.

The great skill and challenge for leaders today is to identify the barriers. All your efforts to collaborate will be futile if barriers don't get torn down. At the same time, you don't want to create a solution for a barrier that doesn't exist.

Q: What are some behaviors leaders can exhibit to help foster a more collaborative culture?

A: First, leaders need to redefine success. Let's take the head of sales in a company. Traditionally, this executive is measured by how much his or her team sells, and if you are that leader, it's the only thing you care about. But when you start working across an organization, with marketing or product development, you need to redefine success. You need to put yourself in the shoes of these other people to understand their interests along with your own, and find a common agenda. It's difficult, but the art is in redefining success away from your own narrow self interest to a bigger goal.

The second behavior leaders should model is to actively engage people and involve them in the process of making decisions. So assume that you only exhibit the first behavior—redefining success to set a common agenda—but then you don't involve people in creating the strategies and action plans needed to achieve that agenda. You're not really collaborating. One of the great things about collaboration is that you bring people with different experiences and different expertise together. There is power in that complementary expertise. So if you can engage people and harness that power by involving them early on when you make decisions, you're going to make better decisions.

The third leadership behavior is demanding extreme accountability. A big problem with collaboration is that it can lead to free-riding or shirking if no one is in charge. You need crystal clear accountability from every team member. What is your responsibility? What are you going to deliver? What are you going to own? If you don't have that, it becomes a complicated and diluted effort.

A fourth leadership skill, which I am researching with a colleague at INSEAD, Herminia Ibarra, is something we call the global connector role. Executives need to broaden their networks and become connectors, so they can get exposure to all kinds of people—in different countries, in emerging markets, in adjacent industries or in different trade organizations. The goal is to be out there so you're able to collect and interpret signals and ideas and bring them back to your organization. This leads to better collaboration because it can help you see a broader range of opportunities.

Encouraging Your People to Share

Once you have embraced a collaborative way to lead, it's time to get others to do the same. Here are some steps you can take to move your organization in a more collaborative direction:

Remove traditional knowledge-sharing barriers.

Collaborative leaders encourage people to share knowledge freely. They recognize and reward employees for facilitating the flow of information rather than obstructing it. You want ideas to travel not only from top to bottom, but also laterally, between and among employees, customers, suppliers, partners and even—sometimes—competitors. Use information technology to connect as many people, in as many places, to as much information as possible. And then understand how people will use these networks of collaboration—usually in short bursts of nonlinear and asynchronous communication.

It's not just homage to Facebook; experts exist in your organization, and those experts are highly valuable in solving your problems as well as those of your customers. And technology makes it possible to place those experts directly into your customer conversations, even when those customers are in entirely different time zones. You can bring those experts to the forefront by creating and nurturing communities of interest. Sometimes those experts exist in trade organizations, academic institutions or user groups. Customers may know your products better than you know them. In fact, Cisco's highest rated customer-service options are self-service. Invite your customers to participate in communities that you host and reward or recognize their contributions. Share opinions, advice and assistance as often as, or more often, than you receive them.

Focus on what gets done, not where and when it gets done. We all know that regular office hours and location-dependent processes are no longer necessarily the norm. Talented, productive individuals need not work under the same roof at the same time in order to collaborate. Some prefer a traditional office environment, but many high-performing people work best from home or other locations, or need increased mobility to match their needs and lifestyles.

In a networked organization that uses collaborative tools,

you can focus on what gets done, and not fixate on where and when it happens. Embrace the flexibility of connected organizations and empower people to achieve a better work/life balance. Then closely monitor how they perform.

It's also important to allow people to express themselves. Keep an open mind to alternative or divergent views and different working styles, and you'll benefit from increased creativity, productivity, loyalty and employee satisfaction.

Set up cross-functional teams that collaborate internally to improve your ability to compete externally. If you are organized in discrete profit-and-loss centers, cross-organizational strategies can be difficult to achieve. As organizations focus more and more on cultivating distinctive centers of value, that value increasingly cuts across and involves multiple functions or business units.

EXPERT TIP ON "SILO SYNDROME"

"When 'silo syndrome' infects an organization, one symptom is finger pointing. If a business unit leader fails to meet gross-margin targets, he or she may insist the problem is that the purchasing group failed to buy materials at the right price. Or, he or she might blame the problem on incompetence within the accounting function. Often the real problem is a lack of collaboration among people in multiple functions and business units whose complementary skills are necessary to create value."

—from *The Culture of Collaboration* by Evan Rosen, Red Ape Publishing, 2009

We have found that when teams that historically competed internally begin working together, the most effective way to turn their energies collectively toward external competition is to define the difference between collaboration and command and control and prepare them to expect either approach depending on what the situation calls for. From our experience, the beginning stages of a cross-organizational initiative call for the greatest degree of collaboration, particularly when teams are establishing a shared vision of success and determining the best strategy to achieve that vision. The closer you get to actually executing the strategy, the more you may need a prescriptive, hierarchical approach to drive accountability and rewards.

In situations when time is short, such as during a crisis or while addressing a critical market opportunity, command and control may be the only option. Know and communicate to your teams the differences between these two approaches, and be clear they should expect either one depending on what's most appropriate. Collaboration brings out the best ideas; sometimes command and control is the best way to execute those ideas.

If you want to become a chief catalyst for collaboration, you need to embrace all of these behaviors. Take a critical look at the way you work. What personal barriers do you need to overcome to better develop a collaborative culture in your company?

60 SECOND WRAP

:00 Culture is the DNA of an organization and an essential pillar that anchors every successful collaboration strategy.

:10 Collaborative organizations thrive on a culture of openness, flexibility and shared goals.

:30 Establishing a collaborative culture takes a sustained commitment by senior leadership.

Collaborative leaders embrace four behavior traits. They:

01 Focus on authentic leadership and eschew passive aggressiveness

02 Relentlessly pursue transparent decision making

03 View resources as instruments of action, not as possessions

04 Codify the relationship between decision rights, accountability and rewards

:50 Encourage your people to support a culture of sharing by:

01 Removing traditional knowledge-sharing barriers

02 Supporting open, flexible working styles

03 Setting up cross-functional collaborative teams

3

GET REAL ABOUT COMMUNICATION

Develop an organization of authentic communicators to fuel effective collaboration.

(ONE REQUIREMENT FOR SUCCESS)

AUTHENTIC

COLLABORATIVE

COMMUNICATORS

EXECUTIVE SUMMARY

Collaborative teams work best when they're made up of people who communicate openly. When you are authentic in your communications, others are as well. This empowers everyone to play to their strengths and maximizes your collective potential.

As people increasingly interact virtually, it becomes even more important to communicate authentically. Collaboration tools constantly improve, making it easier for people to bond even though they're not face to face. But it's hard to be authentic if you aren't aware of your genuine communication style. Learn about your style, and those of others, and you'll communicate more effectively, reach agreement faster and work better together.

Clear and open communication has always been essential to success in the workplace. It becomes more essential all the time as work interactions increasingly occur over video and other technologies. New technology makes it easier to reach people across an organization and around the world. But it does not make it easier to say what you mean and mean what you say.

Collaboration puts our personal communication skills to the test as we cross departmental, cultural and time-zone boundaries. More and more, we work with people we have never met. They live in places we have never seen, and speak languages we do not understand. Teams form, disband and reconfigure at a dizzying pace to keep up with changes in the marketplace. Trust is more important than ever and moving forward, global collaborative teams will be bonding via video.

Given this new virtual business reality—with all the space, time and distance between you and your collaboration partners—how do you find the common ground that enables teams to perform? Start with yourself. Learn how to be an authentic communicator, and then coach others to do the same. Tell people how you make decisions. Let them know your strengths and weaknesses. Share with them who you really are, and they will feel comfortable doing so as well.

Let's begin with a few questions: How do you process information, and how does that affect the way you *communicate* your ideas? When you convey information, do you start with specifics and work your way up to a conclusion? Or do you first establish overarching principles and general truths before you go into the details? Do you draw energy from collaborating with others, or do you enjoy working by yourself and then communicating once you have worked through your thought process? Imagine how much faster your teams could get things done if they knew these answers about you and each other.

The following self-assessment reveals how you process information and how you communicate that information to others. Even better, do the online self-assessment featured in the "Discover Your Style" sidebar. See how much you can learn about yourself—and what surprising discoveries you can make about the people you work with every day.

TEST YOURSELF *Take a quick online self-assessment and receive a customized, complimentary report detailing your unique style.*

DISCOVER YOUR STYLE

Cisco, in partnership with Oregon State University, created the methodology behind the assessment, which is similar in concept to the Myers Briggs personality test. To take the assessment, go to *collaborativecommunicator.com/yourstyle* and click on "Take Survey" in the Be Self Aware box.

Consider a few guidelines before you dive in: When learning about your personal communication style, your goal should not be to change it but to improve how you apply your natural tendencies and strengths in a variety of situations with different kinds of people. The secret is to communicate to people that you're comfortable being yourself, and that you are open, grounded and genuine in the way you communicate.

The best communicators are confident in who they are and allow others a peek inside. Their persona stays the same, no matter who their audience is. Embrace your strengths, acknowledge your shortcomings and you'll earn the trust of your team and pave the way for better collaboration.

The real power we wield is in our authenticity.

Remember that whatever choices you make, some people will agree with them and others will not. Hold your ground. If you are consistent in your principles, you'll be a leader others want to follow.

Here's the reward: When you are genuine and open, you allow others to be so as well. The result of better, more open communication is an increased ability to consider a broader set of perspectives that can help teams make the necessary mid-course corrections and adapt more quickly to opportunities and challenges.

AUTHENTIC COMMUNICATION FUELS EFFECTIVE COLLABORATION

Above all, remember this: You can be a better leader and collaborator if you do one very simple thing—be yourself. The real power we wield as communicators is in our authenticity. So who are you, and what's your unique communication style? It's time for some self-discovery.

The Way We Are

There are many ways we can describe human behavior. When it comes to processing and communicating information, four factors matter most: how your mind processes information, how your mind organizes information, how comfortable you are expressing yourself and how you "connect the dots" for people.

MODEL FOR AUTHENTIC COMMUNICATION

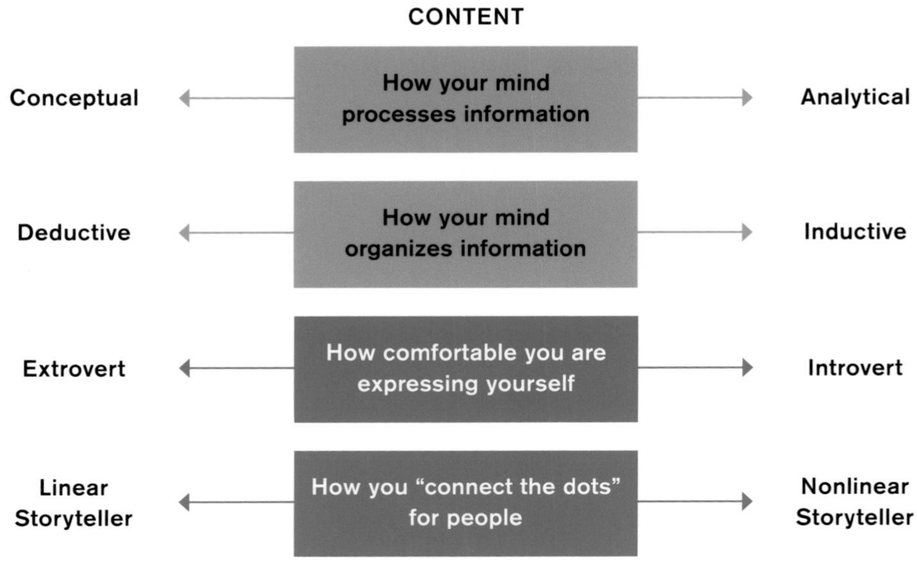

The *Content* side of things refers to the way you naturally think. The *Delivery* side refers to the way you communicate those thoughts to others. Before diving into each element, remember that no style is better or worse than any other. What's important is to understand who you are, so you can embrace your strengths and be more aware of your limitations.

And one more thing: These dimensions are not binary—you're not either/or. In each of the four dimensions, we all have a tendency towards one or the other, but can readily adapt when needed. We are all a little bit of both. We just lean to one side.

Cisco developed this model for authentic communication in conjunction with researchers at Oregon State University. To date, more than 15,000 people have taken the online self-assessment and their feedback indicates that more than 98 percent believe it accurately captures their unique communication style.

EXPERT TIP ON COLLABORATIVE COMMUNICATION

"Collaboration is like a marriage. When you combine awareness of your own strengths and preferences with insight and respectful appreciation for the strengths and preferences of your collaboration partners, you can work together to overcome formidable obstacles and achieve great things. But without that self-awareness, appreciation and respect, it's a recipe for dysfunction and divorce."

—Brad Holst, Mandel Communications

How Do You Process Information?

Do you break problems into pieces and components? Study detail? Understand the working parts? If so, you are probably an *analytical* thinker. Do you like to look at every problem as a whole? Feel better with a big-picture approach? Make easy analogies? If yes, chances are you're a *conceptual* thinker.

As an analytical thinker, you easily remember facts and details. You're also quite good at spotting challenges or obstacles that might be lurking on the horizon. On the down side, it can be easy for you to get so focused on the details that you miss the larger story all together.

If you're a conceptual thinker, you find the story in what you see and hear. You remember ideas easily and like to sniff out opportunities. But your worldview may miss important details and logistics. You may also minimize or fail to pick up on some of the obstacles that could block the way forward.

The conceptual thinker brings ideas to the table and the analytical thinker brings details that ground those ideas in reality.

Analytical thinkers tend to express themselves in *logical narrative*: A leads to B, which leads to C. They process information and get their ideas across using facts, figures, hypotheses and equations. Analytical thinkers come to the meeting armed with road maps and data. They choose precise language, and their approach is accurate and concrete.

Analytical thinkers can improve their communication by recognizing that judgment and gut feeling can also be valuable when making a case, and that others at the table may be waiting to hear the meaning of it all.

Conceptual thinkers, on the other hand, grasp the big picture and visualize the ideal end state. They energize brainstorming sessions and shape new ideas. Conceptual thinkers synthesize data and details into a meaningful whole.

They tell stories in ***symbolic narrative***, using tools like analogies, metaphors and historical comparisons to get ideas across. For presentations, conceptual thinkers build information around a theme—perhaps from a movie, a book or a song—and this establishes a point of connection with their audience.

If you are a conceptual thinker, the analytical people you collaborate with will appreciate some facts and details about processes, milestones and deadlines. They will want to see some due diligence, please.

Strong presenters take advantage of their natural tendencies, but they are prepared to switch gears to address things in a way that makes sense to those with contrasting communication styles. For example, a conceptual thinker might say, "In this presentation, I'm going to tell a story that will help you to visualize the big-picture points I want to make. I'll stop regularly to take questions. I've got all the facts and data that support the presentation, and I am happy to get as detailed as you like."

TEST YOURSELF *Fill in the dot to indicate your preference.*

WHAT IS YOUR PREFERENCE?

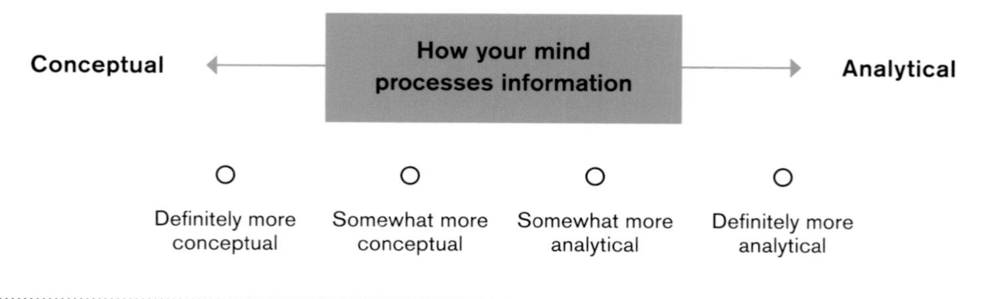

These tendencies don't change when you're communicating virtually. In fact, collaboration technologies and social media allow you to support your natural communication style in new ways. Conceptual thinkers can easily share video clips and other audio-visual cues to build on their themes, and analytical thinkers can share data in graphically compelling ways. Collaboration technologies such as video present new opportunities to enhance your authentic communication style.

How Do You Organize Information?

When you're communicating, either informally or while presenting to an audience, do you prefer to lead with your big idea or recommendation? Do you give the answer first, and then share how you got there? If so, you may be a *deductive* thinker. Deductive people get right to the point and benefit from a formal structure that maps out how they organize information. There's a good chance that you fall into this category as many executives have evolved into deductive thinkers simply because of the demands on their schedules.

Deductive thinking is great for no-nonsense meetings. But when you lead with the answer, you run the risk of quickly polarizing the audience. Others may be quick to voice concerns and share their points of view. You will need to anticipate this response, listen to others and explain how you arrived at your conclusion.

It may not create a lot of mystery or suspense—the hallmarks of great storytelling—but you will find many situations in which a deductive, get-right-to-the-point style is the best approach. Examples include briefing a colleague on the progress of a new initiative, conducting an operational review or any time you are delivering information that might be difficult to hear.

THE REAL
WE WIELD
OUR AUTH

POWER

IS IN

ENTICITY.

At the other end of the spectrum is the communicator who likes to guide people with a story that builds to the preferred conclusion, laying out information and details in a certain sequence. These types of communicators are *inductive* thinkers.

An inductive approach is particularly effective when you are exploring a need or opportunity. It also works well as a way to provide instruction or motivate a team around a new initiative. If you're inductive, you'll find that setting up a thematic structure feels like a natural way to organize thoughts.

For example, salespeople are often trained to use inductive strategies. They don't want to lead with a hypothesis, only to find people in the audience with opposing ideas or immediate objections.

On the other hand, sometimes inductive thinkers will find the audience squirming as they wait for you to get to the point. Some listeners like to cut to the chase, and all the great storytelling in the world won't satisfy them.

TEST YOURSELF *Fill in the dot to indicate your preference.*

WHAT IS YOUR PREFERENCE FOR ORGANIZING INFORMATION?

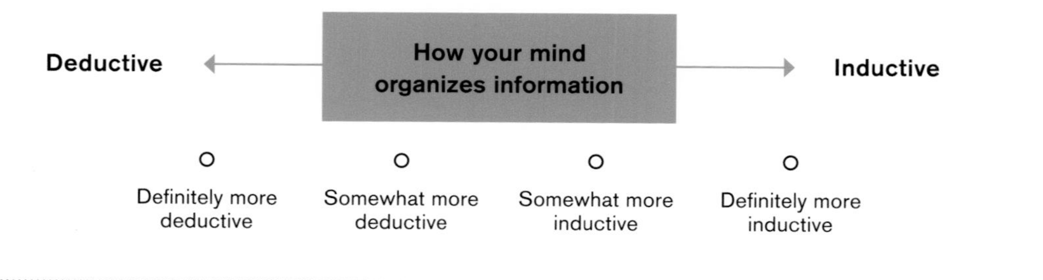

When you're communicating virtually, it becomes even more important to declare how you communicate to set the proper expectations with others. People's attention spans can be even shorter when you're not in the same physical location and able to read body language and other non-verbal cues. If you're clear that you're inductively building to your conclusion—or that you plan to get right to the point—people will adjust and be more receptive.

Are You an Introvert or Extrovert?

There's a quick way to find out if you prefer *extroverted* or *introverted* expression. If you are energized by interactions with others, especially groups of people, you're likely extroverted. And if you are more stimulated by your inner thoughts and ideas, preferring time alone and one-on-one conversations, you're probably introverted.

The biggest challenge for extroverts is an obvious one: learning not to dominate listeners or create an environment that shuts down communication, especially from their introverted colleagues. An extrovert can become a good listener through self-awareness, practice and discipline, but it rarely comes naturally. The tendency—when not actually talking—is to focus more on what to say next rather than actively listening to what others are saying.

To leverage your communication strengths as an extrovert, invite interaction. Ask questions of your listeners to get them involved. Use gestures and move through the room to engage your listeners. Pepper your talk with stories, anecdotes and humor.

One of the great strengths of introverted communicators is that when they speak, people listen. Introverts take the time and focus their energy to tune in to what's being said and how it's being said. Introverts rarely waste time with small talk or thinking out loud. They plan their communications and tailor them to bring value to the listener.

Introverts usually won't interrupt or rush someone else's answer, which gives others space to share their thinking. But don't assume because introverts are quiet that they agree with you. The challenge for introverts, especially in group settings, is to speak up. If you're an introvert, don't hesitate to share your ideas. Everybody benefits when you do.

Communicating virtually raises unique challenges for both extroverts and introverts. Because you're not all together in one room, extroverts won't be able to read the group's reaction as readily and will need to be even more careful not to monopolize the discussion, which can cause other participants to tune out. Introverts have to recognize opportunities to jump in to the discussion more decisively.

Remember, neither an introverted nor extroverted communication style is better than the other. Everyone has the potential to be an excellent communicator.

TEST YOURSELF *Fill in the dot to indicate your preference.*

HOW COMFORTABLE ARE YOU EXPRESSING YOURSELF?

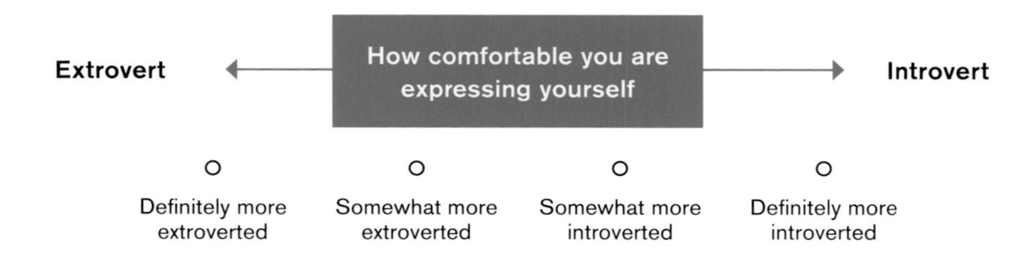

Are You a Linear or Nonlinear Storyteller?

We all tell stories, and the better we tell them, the more clearly we communicate. Listen to people, and you'll find there are two types of storytellers, *linear* and *nonlinear.* Do you prefer to stick to a tightly focused script or agenda with prescribed roles? If so, chances are you're a linear storyteller. Do you like to keep things loose and go off script as the need dictates? That's a good sign that you are a nonlinear storyteller.

TEST YOURSELF *Fill in the dot to indicate your preference.*

HOW DO YOU CONNECT THE DOTS FOR YOUR AUDIENCE?

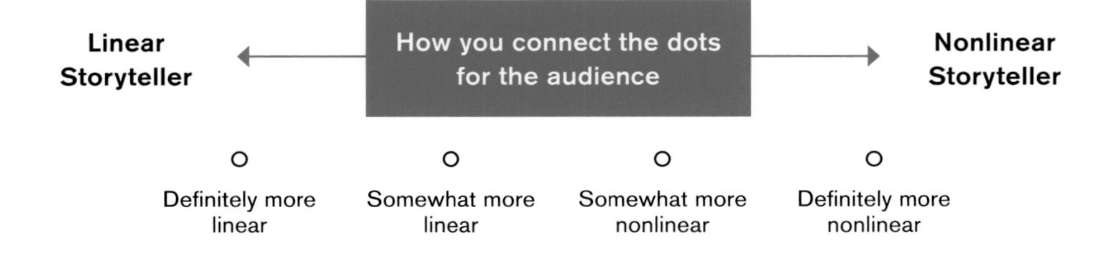

If you are a linear storyteller, you can improve your communication by asking yourself how you manage your communication rhythm. Using an agenda, a timer and tightly prepared notes help you feel confident and natural. But recognize that interruptions can frustrate you, so prepare for and get comfortable with them.

The key to being an effective nonlinear storyteller is to trust and manage your spontaneity, because you will find

AUTHENTIC COMMUNICATION AT A GLANCE

The information on these two pages provides a visual overview of the four most common communication types, as well as information on how to communicate effectively with each one.

In the remainder of the chapter, we discuss ways in which you can successfully "bridge" between styles as you communicate with other people.

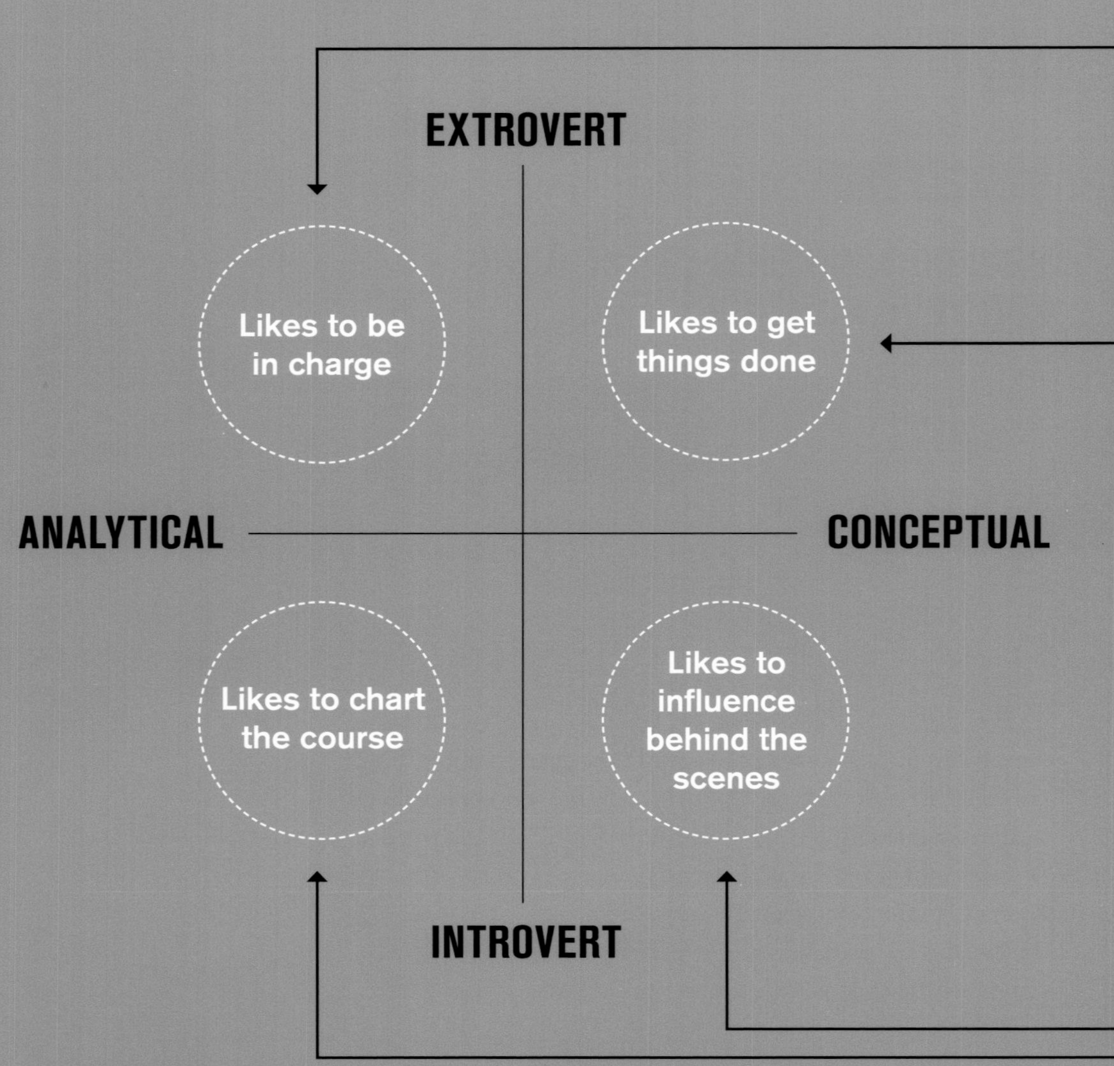

ANALYTICAL / EXTROVERT

Comfort Zone: Talking about results, getting things done

Delivery Cues: Overtly confident; Quick and forceful

Content Cues: Direct, accurate, factual; Bias for action

To Bridge Between Styles

→ Get to the point quickly, then provide logical, factual key assertions

→ Stress compatibility with their goals and practicality

→ Show your conviction; Match their energy

CONCEPTUAL / EXTROVERT

Comfort Zone: Talking about ideas, vision, strategy

Delivery Cues: Outgoing, enthusiastic and often spontaneous

Content Cues: Focused on the big picture; Rarely bogged down with detail; Uses stories, analogies and/or humor

To Bridge Between Styles

→ Keep up with their conversational pace and digressions

→ Focus on concepts/trends and their potential future impact

→ Don't over-focus on details or they will lose interest

ANALYTICAL / INTROVERT

Comfort Zone: Talking about plans, process, details

Delivery Cues: Reserved, speaks in language that is factual and specific

Content Cues: Methodical, organized, well prepared to bridge between styles

To Bridge Between Styles

→ Use factually accurate, detailed information

→ Communicate at a pace that allows time to process and evaluate information

→ When communicating change, present as far in advance as possible

CONCEPTUAL / INTROVERT

Comfort Zone: Talking about theories, strategies, concepts

Delivery Cues: Projects a calm and detached demeanor (may mask true conviction); Uses powerful metaphors

Content Cues: Full of ideas, shares with discretion; Future focused

To Bridge Between Styles

→ Try meeting one-on-one; allow time necessary to establish trust

→ Relate the impact of the ideas to the future; Allow time to ponder ideas and recommendations

→ Be sincere without pretense

yourself going off script.

Use caution not to drift off-message so much that you lose your audience or run out of time. This is a particular concern for extroverted nonlinear storytellers.

One of the biggest myths about nonlinear storytellers is that that they don't need to prepare—they can just wing it. Not true. Plan ahead, but trust that ideas will come to you spontaneously and be ready to roll with them as they come.

Tune into your colleagues' communication styles and you significantly increase the odds of making a meaningful connection.

Understanding your natural tendencies helps you become a more effective communicator. Collaboration flourishes when everyone in an organization knows how best to share his or her ideas and opinions with the group.

Play to Your Strengths, Understand Theirs

Everyone provides cues to his or her authentic communication style. Some are verbal, some non-verbal. By noticing these cues, you can find ways to bridge the differences between another person's style and yours and increase the odds of making a meaningful connection.

The easiest way to assess someone's style is to observe the cues that indicate the two most obvious preferences: *Analytical* or *Conceptual* thinking and *Extroverted* or *Introverted* expression. Using this method, you only have to determine how someone fits into one of four overarching profiles instead of 16 individual ones:

1. *Analytical Introvert — The Planner*
2. *Conceptual Introvert — The Influencer*
3. *Analytical Extrovert — The Leader*
4. *Conceptual Extrovert — The Starter*

How can you tell? There are three types of cues:

→ *Communication comfort zone.* Do your colleagues talk about vision or results? Details or strategies? When do they feel most comfortable during a conversation?

- → ***Delivery cues.*** Look at the way in which they communicate. Are they confident and forceful, or reserved and calm? These are physical cues that show interest.
- → *Content cues.* Do they get excited about details or big ideas? Gathering groups together or marching on alone? What tops their agenda, and what do they leave out?

See if you can guess the communication profile of each of these people as an *Analytical Introvert, Analytical Extrovert, Conceptual Introvert* or *Conceptual Extrovert.*

Role Play 1

You log into a web conference a couple of minutes early, and your colleague is already there. You're greeted in a polite, professional manner and then it's right down to business. Ms. G. says...

> I'm glad you and I could talk in advance of the leadership meeting. Everything has to go right. I went through your slide deck a couple of times. Why don't you start by taking me through how you arrived at the budget calculations? Then let's drill down into the project timeline you provided and make sure it's 100 percent realistic. Finally, I'd like to talk through the details on how you plan to present this recommendation at the meeting.

Did you notice?

- → The communication comfort zone was talking about planning and details.
- → The delivery was professional and somewhat reserved.
- → The content stressed a methodical need to be well prepared and accurate.

The envelope please: If you guessed *Analytical Introvert*, you are correct. People with a preference for Analytical Introverted communication are natural planners. They like to chart the course for a team.

There are three ways to bridge to their style:

→ Use factually accurate, detailed information and organize it in a logical flow.

→ Communicate at a pace that allows them to digest the information. Don't rush the conversation.

→ When communicating change, give them time to process by presenting the recommendation as far in advance as possible.

Role Play 2

You arrive at Mr. D.'s office for a meeting. His head is down and he is working on his laptop—deep in thought. At first, he seems a little distracted by your presence. Then he smiles sincerely and says...

> I appreciate your taking time to meet with me one-on-one. I know we have a team meeting next week, but big groups can be so tiresome. I've been mulling this over for quite a while. Your proposed strategy meets most of the immediate needs quite nicely, but I'm concerned about where we will likely be 12 to 18 months out.

Did you notice?

→ The communication comfort zone was talking about strategies and theories.

→ The delivery seemed distracted at times, but was sincere and the demeanor was calm.

→ The content focused on the future.

Our sample subject was a *Conceptual Introvert*. These

people are natural influencers in their organizations, and often play a big role behind the scenes. They like to set strategy and provide long-term direction.

There are three ways to bridge to their style:

- → Know that they are best persuaded one-on-one, and it takes time to establish trust.
- → Emphasize the future impact and value of anything you discuss.
- → Be yourself. These people in particular lack pretense and appreciate that in others.

Role Play 3

The handshake is firm and the eye contact is piercing. Without any small talk, Ms. K. says...

> I only have 15 minutes, so let's get right down to business. That should be more than enough time for what we need to do. My chief of staff can provide any details and logistical information you need. There are three things I need you to do for me. First, and most importantly, I need your promise that you and your team can make this initiative happen on time, at budget and with minimal business interruption.

Did you notice?

- → The communication comfort zone was all about results and getting things done.
- → The delivery seemed overtly confident.
- → The content was direct and specific.

You are correct if you guessed *Analytical Extrovert.* People with this preference like to be in charge. Senior executives often adopt this style in meeting situations to protect their time and goals, regardless of their natural preference.

1 2 3 4 5 6 7 8 9 10

There are three ways bridge to their style:

- → Take a deductive approach. Get to your point quickly and then be ready to back it up.
- → Stress alignment and compatibility with their goals to hold their attention.
- → Express conviction and urgency for whatever you are discussing.

Role Play 4

A couple of minutes after the meeting was *supposed* to start, the telepresence screens come to life and Mr. B. greets you warmly, like you're old friends. You notice there are three others present who weren't on the meeting invitation. He says...

> Sorry we're late. My last meeting went long. It seems like they've been going long all day. I asked a few members of my team to join us. I'm really excited about the potential of this project and have a number of ideas about how we can kick it off. Maybe we can do some brainstorming while we're all together? By the way, in my last meeting, someone mentioned that you'd taken an innovative approach to one of the challenges my group is also facing. Can we talk a bit about that too?

Did you notice?

- → The communication comfort zone focused on ideas and how to get them off the ground.
- → Delivery seemed friendly and enthusiastic.
- → The content was big picture—no mention of details—and rather spontaneous.

Our test subject here is a *Conceptual Extrovert.* People with this profile love to get things started. Their strong point is kicking off new initiatives.

There are three ways to bridge to their style:

→ Keep up with their conversational pace and be flexible about topics that may come up.
→ Allow time to brainstorm and discuss ideas.
→ Try to keep it big picture. Don't push for details or they will quickly lose interest.

Once you're fluent in identifying styles, you can adjust your own approach to resonate with others and present information in a way that makes a strong connection. The challenge is to make adjustments without sacrificing your authentic style. Stay true to yourself and empower others to do the same. You'll find that people bring better and more diverse ideas to the table and work together more openly and quickly to achieve the results you're after.

EXPERT TIP ON BRIDGING STYLES

"All too often, differences in communication style create a divide between people who need to collaborate together. The best collaborators bridge that divide by adapting their style a bit to accommodate the preferences of others."

—Brad Holst, Mandel Communications

60 SECOND WRAP

:00 Trust among team members is essential to collaboration, yet harder to establish in a virtual environment where teams form rapidly and fluidly.

:05 The way you communicate determines how well you collaborate—and the same goes for your teams.

:15 The first step to improving communication is to identify your unique style for processing and communicating information.

:20 Each personality type has strengths and limitations. The idea is not to change your style, but to make the most of who you naturally are.

:25 Analytical thinkers break problems into pieces and components and understand the working parts, while conceptual thinkers look at every problem as a whole and prefer a big-picture approach.

:30 A deductive approach to communication is great for no-nonsense meetings. An inductive approach is particularly effective when you are exploring a need or opportunity.

:35 To leverage your communication strengths as an extrovert, invite interaction. The challenge for introverts, especially in group settings, is to speak up.

:45 If you are a linear storyteller, use an agenda, a timer and a tight outline to help you feel confident and natural. For nonlinear storytellers, learn to trust and manage your spontaneity.

:55 Identifying the processing and communication style of others will help you build open, trusting teams that bring their best ideas and effort to collaborative initiatives.

4

CREATING COMMITMENT TO SHARED GOALS

Use a common vocabulary to get collaborative teams aligned and working toward a shared vision of success.

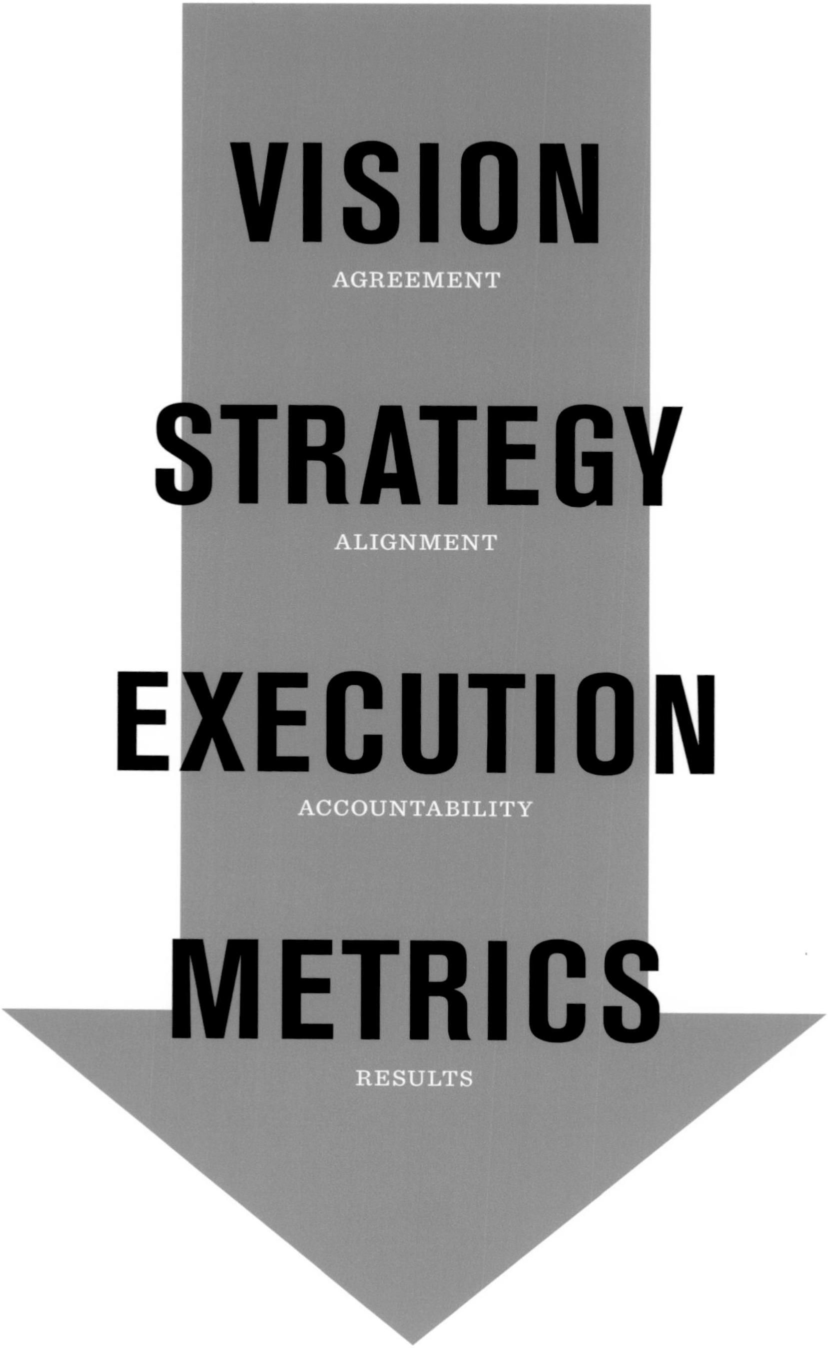

VISION

AGREEMENT

STRATEGY

ALIGNMENT

EXECUTION

ACCOUNTABILITY

METRICS

RESULTS

EXECUTIVE SUMMARY

When everyone speaks the same language, it's a lot easier to keep collaborative teams on track to achieve results. Establishing a common vocabulary for how you communicate decisions and identify the people accountable for the outcomes of those decisions will minimize second guessing and confusion so teams can move faster.

Here is an all-too-familiar situation: A business strategy session wraps up, and you leave the meeting with a sense of direction and positive energy about the plan. Over the next few weeks, enthusiasm wanes, people get distracted and results feel out of reach. What happened?

Most likely, the team as a whole did not uniformly understand or agree with the vision and strategy for the initiative. Most team members probably tried to execute on the strategy to the best of their understanding, while others second-guessed the approach and quietly opted not to commit resources to get the job done. Failure is almost inevitable.

Imagine this scenario played out in a different way: During the meeting, participants all agree to a vision of what success looks like, establishing a *cause* to which employees can apply their passion and sense of purpose, and motivating them to invest discretionary effort—to go the extra mile.

But it doesn't end there. Next, they work together to get aligned and chart a strategy to attain the goal. Then they outline the steps needed to execute on the strategy and map out a framework for measuring the results of their efforts. They capture these decisions on a single slide and assign owners to each deliverable to ensure clear accountability. Having a clear sense of the strategic vision and what's expected of them, team members stay focused on their individual tasks for the duration of the project. Most important, they deliver the target results.

Why do we so often find ourselves in the first situation, when we'd rather be in the second? Powerful collaboration works when teams agree about a vision of what success looks like, get aligned around the best strategies to achieve that vision and clearly understand what actions are required and who is accountable for their execution.

This approach becomes even more important as teams are increasingly made up of people who've never met or worked together before. They may be from different departments and located in different parts of the world, have been educated at different schools and received different training. Often these teams are expected to form, deliver, disband and reconfigure over and over to adapt, solve problems and move the business forward faster. When these teams get stuck, the reason is often a lack of clarity around their purpose and end goals.

The Importance of a Common Vocabulary

Establishing a common vocabulary for decision making helps teams to articulate their goals and commit to the approach they'll follow to achieve them. It is a valuable process in making a collaborative culture operational and makes teams more adaptable and agile.

Try this experiment: Ask a colleague to define your company strategy. Then ask someone else. Chances are, you'll hear variations on a theme: satisfy customers, lower costs, beat a competitor. These all may be valid strategies. But each employee has learned a slightly different interpretation along the way.

It's difficult enough to gain commitment to a strategy across a small team, let alone an entire organization, unless everyone shares a common understanding of the goals and how to achieve them. In a collaborative enterprise, where it's even easier to veer off course, it becomes more important to agree on the meaning of key terms so teams can mobilize, execute and adapt quickly.

As you determine your strategic vision, it's wise to include many voices and perspectives and encourage knowledge sharing, open-mindedness and constructive debate. But once everyone has weighed in, you need agreement on the way forward. At this stage, a common vocabulary for decision making becomes critical. It has to be something that everyone understands, accepts and knows how to measure progress against.

This kind of transparent decision making results in a more resilient and adaptive organization. Give it a try, and you'll find that people spend less time questioning a decision and more energy working to achieve the desired outcomes.

There are two main reasons why teamwork goes bad: First, sometimes people who don't agree with a decision nod their heads during group discussions rather than raise their objection. Only later do they second-guess, ignore or in some way undermine the decision. Second, and more commonly, well intentioned employees—who don't know why or by whom a decision is made and believing they are acting in the company's best interest—question the decision, inadvertently undermining it. It's human nature. When we know how decisions are made, who made them and what the outcomes of those decisions mean, however, we are more likely to accept the choices and get on with our work.

Establishing a common vocabulary that helps leaders consistently define decision-making rights and communicate outcomes is an excellent way to build organizational confidence. This speeds alignment, commitment and action. It may seem obvious, but in our conversations with business leaders, we find that very few companies have actually established a common vocabulary.

Procter & Gamble (P&G) is one company that does this well, having adopted a common vocabulary around the terms *Objectives, Goals, Strategies* and *Measures* (OGSM) to drive its strategic planning process.[2]

While the terms P&G uses vary from those we've adopted at Cisco—we'll get to our common vocabulary shortly—the result is the same: increased agreement, alignment and accountability. The point is not that one set of terms is better than another, but rather that establishing some sort of common vocabulary appropriate for your organization is beneficial. Every company is made up of individuals with different value systems, educations and cultural backgrounds. You have to consider all these factors when creating your company's Esperanto for decision making.

It's important to think through the taxonomy, guiding principles and specific definitions of this common vocabulary. As a leader, you are responsible for deciding what terms should be included, the context in which teams apply the vocabulary and how terms are defined. Take the time to make sure you do this right. Once it's established, you'll find that your common vocabulary takes root and is challenging to adjust. Be thoughtful and get it right the first time.

How Cisco Teams Use a Common Vocabulary to Make Decisions That Stick

Cisco's common vocabulary for making decisions includes four terms: *Vision, Strategy, Execution* and *Metrics* (VSEM). This model works for us, but every company should create

A SUCCES
VISION S
INVOLVES
ART AND

SFUL

ATEMENT

BOTH

SCIENCE.

a vocabulary that reflects its own culture. Our hope is that sharing how Cisco uses our common vocabulary will spur ideas you can apply within your company.

Collaborative teams throughout Cisco use the VSEM common vocabulary to get everyone on the same page. It establishes a consistent understanding about the decisions each team makes concerning its shared vision of success, the strategies it employs to achieve that vision, the execution plans it uses to drive those strategies and how it measures success. As a result, teams more clearly see the decision paths in their collaborative projects and can determine decision-making rights along those paths. They also gain a clear understanding of who is accountable for the outcomes of the decisions. It's important that your common vocabulary is woven into your accountability system to ensure teams move from vision to metrics-driven execution.

Cisco teams commonly publish their VSEM documents internally and share them companywide. Increasingly, the company is embedding the common vocabulary within its performance-management systems, so individuals know what they are accountable for, how they are measured and how their work aligns to the vision of the company.

We have learned that along with the potential benefits of increased collaboration come increased risks. If collaborative efforts are not supported by extremely clear responsibility and accountability parameters, it's easy for people to disengage and hide behind the ambiguity. Collaborative work practices succeed only if you create a culture not only of shared goals but also of shared accountability—one that helps people understand how the collaborative work ties into how they're measured, recognized and rewarded. Without this structure, "opt-out" thinking will undermine collaborative efforts.

So what exactly do the words *vision, strategy, execution* and *metrics* mean at Cisco? Let's learn more about each component of this common vocabulary.

Defining *Vision*

When creating a VSEM common vocabulary for a team, we start with building alignment around a long-term overarching statement that defines what we want the future to look like. This is a team's shared *vision* of success. Of all the words in our VSEM vocabulary, this vision is the most difficult to nail down and also the most important.

For our purposes, a vision is the description of a team's long-term desired outcome that inspires, energizes and helps everyone create a mental picture of the team's target. The words in a vision statement should capture the hearts and minds of team members and offer an enduring idea that galvanizes them to act.

The *vision* represents the successful end state for which you are aiming. It's the future you want to achieve described as if you have already achieved it.

Crafting a vision is not as easy as it may seem. Vision is not a consensus-built, pie-in-the-sky phrase. It is a precise, challenging and consequential shared goal that articulates a purpose. It should also reflect an "outside-in" perspective that's tightly focused on helping internal or external customers address their biggest issues. In this context, the customer could be your company's end customers or, for teams such as IT or logistics with an internal enablement role, the clients within a company that the team supports.

You'll need both art and science to create a vision statement. The art lies in looking into the future to imagine what's possible and painting a compelling picture of what success looks like. At the same time, the vision statement needs to include precise language based in reality—and that's the science. You'll ground your vision in reality by exploring a few questions:

- → What specifically do we want to accomplish?
- → What is our value proposition?
- → What does success look like?
- → Is our vision broad enough to be meaningful?
- → Is it narrow enough to be completed?
- → How would the world be different if our team did not exist?

A clear, easy-to-understand vision statement galvanizes people to get the job done. It encapsulates the shared goals of team members from different departments, companies or organizations. You know you're on the right track when team members think the team's shared vision is bigger than—but not in conflict with—their individual or departmental goals. They can then direct and influence their work according to the agreements they have made in support of the shared vision.

Here's another benefit of a strong vision statement: Research says that employees who are emotionally invested in their work perform better and are more satisfied.[3] What better way to get employees engaged than to share a clear, challenging and inspiring vision that everyone can rally around?

One of the most enduring examples of a great vision comes from the founder of Ford Motor Company in 1909:

To democratize the automobile

Or how about this one from the electronics retailer Best Buy:

To relieve consumer "technostress"

Here's our vision statement at Cisco:

Changing the way we work, live, play and learn

Characteristics of a Great Vision Statement

- → A vivid, idealized and memorable description of a desired outcome
- → Inspiring, energizing and helpful in creating a mental picture of your target
- → Based on an "outside-in" perspective—focused on evolving customer needs rather than an insular, status quo mentality
- → An enduring idea that galvanizes people to get behind something
- → Compatible with the team's agreed-upon goals and direction
- → Something that every team member should be able to recite
- → Broad enough to be meaningful for the entire duration of the team's existence

Use an "Outside-In" Perspective to Evolve with Your Customers

While your shared vision of success is a long-term, enduring expression, it must also evolve as necessary. Consider this recent example of Procter & Gamble.[4] The evolution of P&G's markets—spurred by the emergence of developing countries—caused Chairman and CEO Robert McDonald and his team to rethink the company's vision for future success. P&G wanted to increase its appeal with customers in these markets who are constrained by low income levels. As a result, its vision evolved to "Touching and improving more lives, in more parts of the world, more completely."

How will P&G know if it has accomplished its vision? By measuring how it did in relation to the ambitious target the company set: Acquire 800 million new customers worldwide by 2015. Time will tell whether P&G will rise to the challenge, but creating a clear picture of a successful future motivates the individuals and teams within the company.

Once you get the vision right, the other pieces fall into place. Start with the wrong vision, and it will be impossible to attain the results you desire.

The Collaborative Scale

A common vocabulary aids leaders in identifying where decisions need to be made and who owns decision rights at various points. It can also help you to decide what type of approach will work best for different phases or situations during projects.

From our experience, the beginning stages of a new team or project call for the greatest degree of collaboration. The efforts to discuss and define your team's VSEM should be highly collaborative as differing viewpoints are considered. As you move from collectively establishing the VSEM to individuals and sub-teams actually carrying out the actions that support the decisions made about your vision and strategies, a more prescriptive hierarchy can help to drive accountability and results. Teams agree on a *vision*, align resources with a *strategy* and are held accountable for *execution* through well-publicized *metrics*.

Does this mean that people working on individual execution goals shouldn't collaborate? No. But the time for highly collaborative discussion, debate and decision making around the team's focus is over, and it's time to execute. Their collaboration should focus on working closely with the right people to complete the tasks for which they are accountable.

Defining *Strategy*

The "S" in VSEM stands for *strategy.* If there ever was a term misused in business, it's this one. Strategy is about creating differentiation and competitive advantage. Strategic decisions almost always involve tough trade-offs and being comfortable saying no to the things your company should not do in favor of directing focus and resources to the things it needs to do.

A strategy, or a set of strategies, is a concise definition of how your team will make progress toward your vision. It's the elements or actions that differentiate your team, your goal or your company. Part of your work here is to identify the resources and assets the team needs to enact the strategy.

One big challenge leaders face is getting employees to understand that strategy is about prioritization, sacrifice and focus. Ultimately, there are very few factors that separate misguided strategies from ones that create sustained differentiation in the eyes of your customers or stakeholders. That's why teams should be clear on their organization's strategic orientation and understand its implications before discussing a specific team strategy.

Characteristics of a Great Strategy

- → Provides a concise definition of how your team will make progress toward your vision
- → Usually involves making difficult trade-offs
- → Taps the organizational resources and assets required to get the job done
- → Is targeted and focused—it does not try to be all things to all people
- → Is sustainable for the required length of time
- → Is actionable

Some companies study their competition to determine how best to differentiate themselves. Some zero in on the needs of their customers to inform strategy. Still others focus on their own financial models as expressions of strategy. No orientation is right or wrong; what's important is that you determine the best approach to suit your organization's capabilities and circumstances.

You can create your team's strategy by answering a few questions:

- → What is our organization's strategic orientation (customer needs, operational excellence, competitive differentiation, financial impact and so on)?
- → How, and how well, does our strategy help us achieve our vision?
- → What resources and assets do we have available to enact our strategy?
- → Does our team have the capability and permission to commit these resources?
- → Can we commit these resources until the team's goals are complete?
- → What differentiates us, and how can we maximize that differentiation?
- → Is this strategy actionable? Is it sustainable?

It's important to flesh out strategies with enough detail that they'll be actionable when it comes time to execute and specific enough that individuals or teams can be held accountable for them.

Strategy and the Art of the Tough Trade-Off

Some people believe that being strategic is about being smart but, ultimately, it's more about the ability to make hard choices. If you're looking for a strategic person, it's usually the one who is comfortable saying "no."

Consider this example: In 2007, Netflix, which had made waves with its DVD-by-mail business model, knew that streaming content would eventually render DVDs obsolete.[5] It was on the brink of introducing a Netflix-branded set-top box to stream content to customers. The hardware was developed and the advertising campaign was about to launch, but Netflix founder Reid Hastings was having doubts. If

Netflix's vision was to reach as many viewers as possible, he believed that a software-based solution integrated into multiple devices would be more advantageous than a single, proprietary, Netflix-branded offering.

1 2 3 4 5 6 7 8 9 10

EXPERT TIP ON STRATEGY

"If you are not genuinely pained by the risk involved in your strategic choices, it's not much of a strategy."

—Netflix Founder Reid Hastings, *Fortune Magazine*, December 6, 2010

The company did some tough soul-searching and decided against launching the Netflix-branded device, pivoting instead to a software-only strategy. Was it easy to shelve the strategy to which it had been committed and spent much money to develop? No way. Was it the right thing to do? Absolutely. As of this writing, Netflix had made another tough trade-off choice, deciding to split itself up into two companies, one for streaming movies and the other for renting DVDs by mail. Time will tell if this strategy pays off.

Best Buy Uses Shared Goals to Meet Customer Needs and Create Better Growth Opportunities

For Best Buy, a leading global consumer electronics retailer, a change in its business provided the ideal motivation to move toward a more collaborative business model grounded in a culture of shared goals.

Best Buy witnessed firsthand the evolution of consumers' interactions with technology products. No longer did customers view TVs, entertainment systems, computers, phones or even home appliances as separate things. Increasingly, these products were blending into a complex composite of networked devices, applications and services to support their digital lives.

"It's about creating an experience," explains Neil McPhail, senior vice president and general manager of New Business Solutions at Best Buy. "It's not about, 'I want a home theater system.' It's 'I want Fridays to be movie night with my daughter or I want to be connected to my friends and family when I'm traveling.' So as your relationship with your customers changes, how do you change as an organization?"

With this question in mind in the summer of 2009, Best Buy CEO Brian Dunn and his team embarked on a transformative journey. The goal was to position the company for future success by doing two things:

→ Use the evolving needs of customers to create a set of shared goals that the entire company rallies around
→ Take a more global approach to the business, both in addressing those customer needs and in tapping into Best Buy's global pool of talent and resources

Dubbed the "Path to the Connected World," Best Buy's new vision helped leaders view success based less on individual product categories and more on the connected experience their customers demanded. In fact, this notion of connectivity inspired one of the biggest shifts for Best Buy.

In the old paradigm, each product category, such as computing or home entertainment, was the focus of an independent merchandising organization responsible for driving revenue growth strictly within its discrete category.

In the new model, Best Buy formed seven Customer Solutions Groups, cross-functional teams of subject-matter experts who collaborate to create a comprehensive picture of the customers' needs. These seven teams identify ways to meet the needs of Best Buy's customers, combining products and services from multiple solutions groups.

"We shifted from focusing on procuring, pricing, merchandising and selling products to building solutions that included products, but that started with what the customer needed from Best Buy and built backward," explains Christine Webster-Moore, vice president of New Business Solutions at Best Buy.

Today, Best Buy expects leaders to act like general managers who watch out for the entire business, instead of line managers who focus only on the success of their specific team, department or product category. "We are all held accountable for the cumulative outcome of the organization, and that's very clear when you look at what we spend managing against that outcome as well as how we prioritize activities," McPhail says.

It takes time to shift a company's culture to one of shared goals. Best Buy continues to refine its processes to facilitate greater collaboration, and the new direction is bearing fruit. "There's a greater willingness to engage in debate as opposed to some of the counterproductive behaviors we saw in the past," Webster-Moore says. "There's more consistency between what is said during the meeting and what happens after the meeting, and more of a 'stick-with-it-ness' when we run into issues. There is a positive and healthy dynamic on the leadership team, and that is a function of both the collaborative structure and the leaders who are in those roles now."

By working together more collaboratively, Best Buy's leaders are creating bigger and better opportunities for the company. "Most, if not all, of the significant growth strategies that Best Buy is embarking on are a result of collaboration by multiple Customer Solutions Groups taking on an unmet consumer need in a new and unique way," McPhail says.

That's really the promise—and the challenge—of collaboration. "The world moves too fast for any one entity to grow and take advantage of the value pool without collaboration," McPhail concludes. "Collaboration will be the point of differentiation between the companies that grow successfully into the next decade and those that don't."

Defining *Execution*

Once you've determined your strategy, you're ready for the execution phase, which involves creating the list of tasks that your team will ultimately carry out.

Execution plans must align with the strategies that support your vision. While your team should have open, collaborative dialogue when you're deciding on the execution plans, once those plans have been determined, the time for questioning and second-guessing should be over, just as it is in the earlier phases of articulating vision and determining strategy.

Execution represents the specific steps you will take in the short term that support the strategies to accomplish your vision.

It's important to assign ownership of execution activities to specific individuals or teams. We've learned that in order to drive commitment and accountability, there has to be a person or group of people who owns each execution activity and is held accountable for making sure the work gets done. As Cisco continues to evolve its alignment from vision through to execution, we are increasingly mapping individuals' goals (often tied to specific execution activities) in our performance management systems to the strategies of their teams. This helps employees to see the clear connection between the strategies their teams decide to pursue and the individual tasks and goals on which they'll be measured. As a common vocabulary is integrated into a rewards and recognition system, employees begin to see more clearly how their direct execution tasks help them develop career success. This is a good example of the culmination of culture, process and technology and the positive impact they can make.

Characteristics of Great Execution Statements

- → Concisely describes the most important functional or cross-functional initiatives, programs or actions the team is pursuing to deliver on each strategy
- → Informs your team's execution plans for the near future

Here are a few questions to help you determine your execution goals:

- → Do our execution plans directly support our vision and strategies?
- → What are the milestones for success?
- → How will we measure our success?
- → Do we have room to improve or evolve the process as we move forward?

Defining *Metrics*

The best vision and strategy will fall short without the accountability that comes with measuring your progress. Metrics reveal what is working, and what is not. If you don't have metrics, you can't measure progress, and if you can't measure progress, you can't claim victory.

Cisco has adopted the well-established Balanced Scorecard approach, which combines a dashboard of financial and non-financial metrics to give managers a complete view of performance progress.[6]

Metrics aren't easy to design. They may differ radically when you are improving a process versus creating a product, for example. But following a four-step process will yield a solid metrics framework every time:

Metrics provide the framework for team and personal accountability.

1) Identify what you're measuring, whether it's financial performance, customer satisfaction, productivity improvements or some other goal
2) Determine a benchmark to measure against
3) Establish performance targets based on the benchmark you've established
4) Measure your performance against your targets

Traditional financial metrics such as revenue, profits, bookings and margins provide an important part of the performance story, but there are other indicators to consider. Customer-based metrics such as customer satisfaction, or your position within a market, can be very helpful, as can metrics focused on operational excellence, such as tracking productivity and cycle times.

Metrics that reveal the overall health trends of the business can be especially telling. Measuring employee confidence, team engagement, talent retention or project cycle times helps you to identify and target improvement areas.

Characteristics of Great Metrics

→ Clearly show how people and teams will be held accountable for the success of the initiatives, programs or actions in measurable terms

→ Describe how results are related to the team's strategies and/or vision

→ Are specific, measurable, agreed-upon, realistic and time-bound

→ Create an operations review process that includes collaboration and business results

→ Drive improvement against performance targets

Sharing Your VSEM

Once you've agreed on a VSEM, whether for a small team or for the entire company, the next step is documenting that information in a template that allows your team and those outside the team to view it. This VSEM template is a declaration of your team goals and commitments and can be summarized on a single presentation slide or one-page document.

Think of a VSEM template as your team's billboard. Use it to foster collaborative behavior across the company.

Sharing your VSEM template is extremely important as you collaborate with other teams and departments. The more that sharing becomes a ritualized part of your culture, the faster you can mobilize your people for focused action and the more pervasive the benefits become. The rise of social media and other modes of rapid information sharing make it easier than ever to get many more people on the same page. Socialize your VSEM with your stakeholders, publish it in on your company's intranet and embed it in your organization's performance-management system, so when employees are creating their goals and objectives for the upcoming year, they do so with your vision, strategy, execution plans and metrics in mind. Nothing motivates people to action better than clear alignment and accountability.

The VSEM becomes a tool for communicating with other business functions, as well as your own team. Try it out and see how quickly you win the support of your peers.

With a VSEM Template in Hand:

- → Employees will understand how their work aligns to the vision and strategies of your team.
- → You and your fellow team leaders will communicate the vision and strategies of your teams and better align execution to strategies.
- → Company spokespeople can use the model to communicate the team's vision and strategy to internal and external audiences.

At Cisco, we use the VSEM template to drive collaboration by enabling teams to consistently communicate and align to:

- → What the team agreed to do together and what the team's shared goals are (*Vision*)
- → How the team prioritizes and allocates resources to achieve the vision (*Strategy*)
- → The three to five key functional or cross-functional

initiatives, programs or actions the team is pursuing to deliver on each strategy (*Execution*)

- → How the team plans to measure success and who will be held accountable to the execution plan (*Metrics*)

VSEM: Getting It Right

You Know You're Succeeding When…

- → You can identify a clear purpose, a compelling direction and a picture of what success will look like.
- → You can identify the unique value of a team over and above individual contributions.
- → Team members understand what ability or role each member brings to the endeavor and the value of these interdependencies.

You Know You're Failing When…

- → Team members cannot articulate your team's vision.
- → Team members do not understand why they were selected for the team or what their role is.
- → It's unclear how the team or individual members measure success.
- → The team can't make decisions that stick.
- → Trust between members is low or inconsistent.

The template is also a great way to communicate with both internal and external audiences. If your team's work is proprietary or sensitive, consider creating two templates:

- → The *alignment template* is for your team's eyes only and includes confidential or detailed information.
- → The *communication template* provides a quick, motivational snapshot of what the team is trying to accomplish

and doesn't include sensitive information, so you can share it widely with confidence.

Vision, strategy, execution and metrics—these comprise the foundation of every collaborative initiative at Cisco. This common vocabulary for decision making is a valuable tool that helps us get—and stay—aligned and focused on shared goals. We hope that learning about our common vocabulary helps you realize the value of establishing one of your own. Now it's your turn.

CREATE A TEMPLATE FOR YOUR COMMON VOCABULARY

When you're done with the process, if you're using Cisco's VSEM approach, your template might look like this:

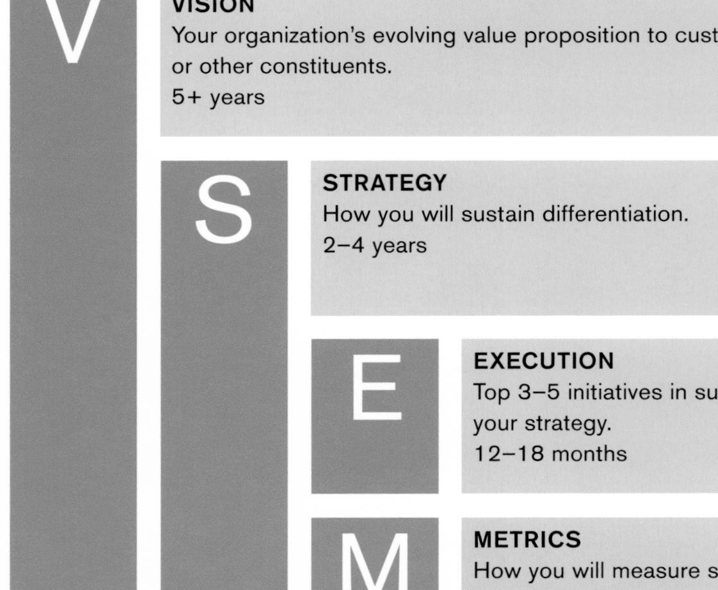

V
VISION
Your organization's evolving value proposition to customers or other constituents.
5+ years
S
STRATEGY
How you will sustain differentiation.
2–4 years
E
EXECUTION
Top 3–5 initiatives in support of your strategy.
12–18 months
M
METRICS
How you will measure success.
12–18 months

60 SECOND WRAP

:00 A common vocabulary goes a long way toward creating alignment, minimizing second-guessing and ensuring collaborative team success.

:10 The common vocabulary also identifies where decisions need to be made and who should make them.

:20 Every organization can benefit from a common vocabulary that reflects its culture and circumstances.

:40 For collaborative teams and projects, Cisco defines four key terms: *vision*, *strategy*, *execution* and *metrics*.

01 Vision: Communicates a team's shared view of success

02 Strategy: Represents key decisions for where/how to apply resources to accomplish the vision

03 Execution: The critical initiatives, programs or actions in support of each strategic priority

04 Metrics: Shows how the team measures success and agrees to be held accountable to the execution plan

:50 A one-page template declares to your team and all stakeholders what you're going to do.

:55 With the action plan in hand, each team member can work toward shared goals, and the team leader can communicate the plan to other groups, facilitating better collaboration across the company.

5

BUILD TEAM TRUST FAST

Help teams overcome the challenges of working virtually to foster the kind of trust and accountability that are essential to collaboration.

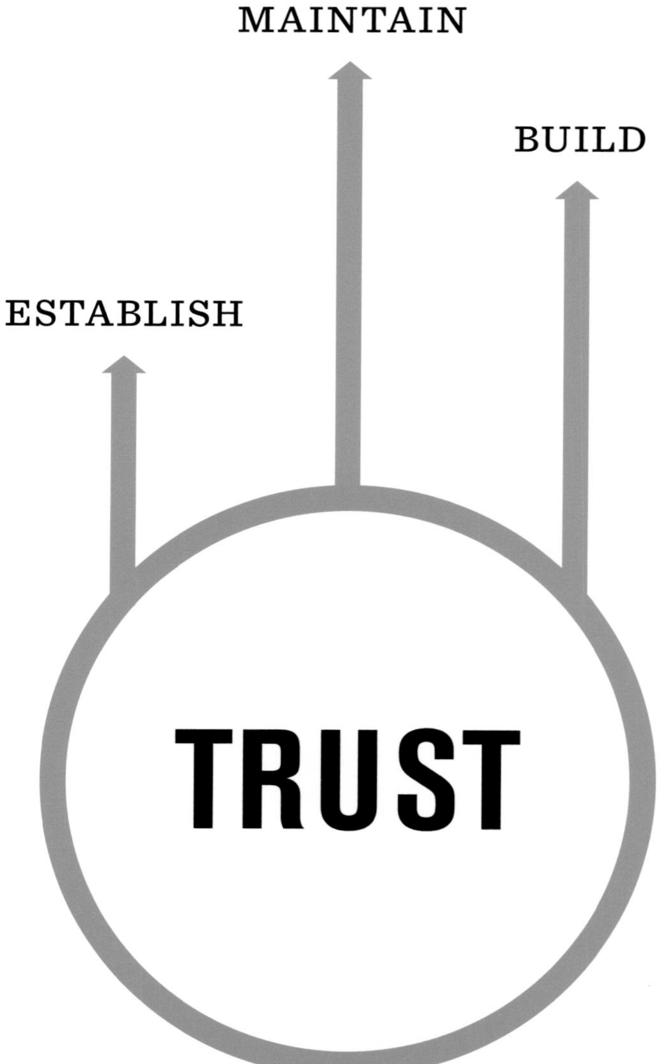

MAINTAIN

BUILD

ESTABLISH

TRUST

EXECUTIVE SUMMARY

Trust anchors every successful collaborative team. And it becomes even more crucial as technology-enabled virtual teams form, disband and re-form to keep up with the pace of business.

But there is a simple way to accelerate the trust-building process—even before your first meeting—and maintain that trust as your team gets down to the work at hand.

Why do some teams exceed all expectations while others never hit their stride? It may come down to trust. An important ingredient in traditional organizations, trust becomes all the more critical when you are working in virtual teams that involve multiple business functions and use video, social media and other collaboration technologies to come together with the goal of getting things done faster.

In a decentralized organization, trust helps you establish norms that minimize individual interpretations of what is appropriate behavior and what is not. When you build trust early and set a precedent of agreement, accountability and achievement, teams produce value that is much greater than the sum of their parts.

How do you encourage trust? Replace uncertainty with clarity. Articulate the team's purpose and establish up front what you expect from each member. You may worry that you don't have time for trust-building exercises. But it's much riskier to skip this step. Invest the time to help teams get acquainted, and the time it takes to generate results will shrink. Small, nimble teams with good chemistry consistently outperform larger, better-resourced teams that lack this kind of trust. And while global, geographically dispersed teams are the new business norm, collaboration technologies such as high-definition video communications and enterprise social software now offer virtual team members great opportunities to make meaningful connections quickly.

Here is a proven technique for building trust: Capture a concrete, precise expression of the team's purpose in a team charter. It will become the focal point around which the team builds trust and healthy collaboration habits.

EXPERT TIP ON BEGINNINGS

> **"Beginnings are incredibly critical periods in the life of any collaborative team. Getting the essentials right from the start increases the chances that you will accomplish your goals and encounter fewer problems."**

—from *Senior Leadership Teams* by Ruth Wageman, Debra A. Nunes, James A. Burress and J. Richard Hackman, Harvard Business Press, 2007

Most of us have been on teams that suffer from a lack of purpose, cohesion or accountability. How about teams plagued by tension and friction? Sometimes team members don't fully engage or work well together. In most cases, it's not because the people don't like each other. They just don't understand how the other team members think and communicate. When you're thrown together as a group of strangers and expected to volunteer your time, skills and experience, it's easy to withdraw. If you can eliminate this uncertainty, a team of people can trust each other and collaborate to achieve successful outcomes together with greater speed.

More than 80 percent of companies cite establishing rapport and trust as a key challenge of working on virtual teams.[7]

Replacing Uncertainty With Trust

How do you replace uncertainty with understanding and trust? Clarify the team's *purpose, role, shared goals* and *scope*. Then capture this information in a team charter. The idea of a team charter is not revolutionary, and there are many ways to go about creating one. The act of creating the charter together with team members is more important than the exact elements you choose to write down. Ideally, teams work with an executive sponsor who helps them create a charter that reflects how their work supports the broader vision and strategies of the company.

Here are the elements that Cisco teams use in their team charters:

- → **Team Purpose:** The team's chartered purpose should describe the specific challenges, opportunities or tasks the team is addressing.
- → **Team Role:** What is the primary role of your overall team—aligning, decision making, executing? The team role is different from the roles and responsibilities of individual team members. Also, your team may play more than one role; just be sure the charter is clear about the scope and time frame of each role.
- → **Shared Goals:** Collaborative teams often bring people together from different departments and functions, each with their own goals and agendas. It's important for individuals to set these aside to a certain degree and reach agreement on a set of shared goals that will benefit the larger organization.
- → **Scope:** Well-defined boundaries narrow the to-do list

> for team members and give them permission to say no to scope creep. The result is projects that stay on track and attain the desired outcome. Scope also helps employees determine the duration of their commitment to ensure that teams don't outlive their value. One of the benefits of a decentralized approach is the ability to act with speed and flexibility when applying an organization's resources to new opportunities. Once a team's work is finished, you'll want to move people onto the next challenge. Being clear about the scope of your team's work helps to determine when the team crosses the finish line.

In addition to determining purpose, roles, goals and scope, your charter should establish *ground rules* that govern how your team will collaborate, as well as *roles* and *responsibilities* for individual team members (which will complement the role of the team as a whole).

As your team works to address these details, a few important things happen. First, uncertainty and anxiety are replaced by understanding and confidence as team members prepare to work together. Second, the process itself provides a natural way for teams to get to know each other and learn about the different personalities, skill sets and experiences of the individuals who are involved. This knowledge informs what roles individuals can play and helps everyone get personally invested in the team's work.

How can you get individuals to do what they say they'll do? Get them personally invested in the team's work and outcomes.

How VSEM and Team Charter Work Together

In the last chapter, we talked about creating a Vision, Strategy, Execution and Metrics (VSEM) common vocabulary for your team. You may wonder how the VSEM and team charter documents fit together. Here's one way to think about it: If a VSEM is about *where we're going,* then a team charter *insures we're moving in the right direction* and *provides the ground rules for getting there.*

Your VSEM should be aspirational and inspirational, painting a picture of what success looks like. The team charter includes details about your specific team's purpose and expectations.

As a leader, you may want teams to establish the VSEM first and let it inform the charters of various teams that support it. Alternately, it may be helpful for teams to create their charters first and let those influence a VSEM. Or you can create the two documents in tandem. There is no correct sequence, and as the leader you should apply these ideas in whatever way makes the most sense for your company.

What Type of Collaborators Are on Your Teams?

One of the things that makes life interesting is the endless variety of people and personalities we encounter. When it comes to working together, that variety can make things more interesting than we'd prefer. In his book *Collaboration*, Dr. Morten T. Hansen identifies four types of workers:[8]

→ **Lone stars:** Workers who deliver successfully on individual goals but exhibit behaviors that run counter to the needs of a team or the collaborative approach an organization is trying to embrace

→ **Butterflies:** Workers who are happy to participate in endless committees or other collaborative groups while their own jobs suffer

→ **Laggards:** People who are not interested in trying anything new and will rebuff any attempt to change the way things are done

→ **T-shaped:** Employees who perform well both in their own jobs and within collaborative teams, (hence the image of a "T," indicating the ability to work vertically and horizontally)

Hansen recommends the development of T-shaped behavior within organizations, but a team charter can help teams succeed no matter what types of workers are involved.

Establishing Ground Rules for Collaboration

Collaboration ground rules are guidelines to help team members know how to treat each other, communicate, participate, cooperate, support each other and coordinate joint activity. They can cover any or all of the following:

- → Team procedures and processes
- → Use of time
- → Use of collaborative technology
- → Meeting preparation and logistics
- → Internal communication
- → Attitudes, respect and courtesy
- → Creativity
- → Participation expectations
- → Problem solving
- → Decision making
- → Conflict resolution

Ground rules must be clear, consistent, agreed upon and, most of all, not forgotten. Your leaders and teams can establish ground rules that best fit your unique organization, but here are some samples to use as a starting point. They are organized into two categories: how people treat each together and how people work together.

How people treat each other:

- → We treat each other with respect.
- → We value constructive feedback.
- → We recognize the accomplishments of both the overall team and its individual members.
- → We emphasize balanced participation and are inclusive of all team members.
- → We give each person a chance to speak while respecting the group's time and the meeting timetables.

- → We emphasize open and honest communication—there are no hidden agendas.
- → We de-personalize debate and discussion of issues—no attacks on people.
- → We listen without judgment and keep an open mind on issues until it is time to decide.
- → When we raise an issue or a problem, we also try to propose a solution.

How people work together:

- → We will hold regular meetings that, if necessary, alternate to accommodate participants in different time zones.
- → The team leader will distribute an agenda no less than 48 hours in advance.
- → Team members are responsible for contacting the team leader to add agenda items.
- → Meetings will start on time.
- → A running list with action items and responsibilities will be maintained, reviewed in meetings and distributed with the meeting minutes.
- → Meeting minutes will be distributed within 24 hours after the meeting.
- → We will use the agreed-upon decision-making model for important decisions and issues.
- → For less important issues, we will rely on the subject-matter expert with input from others.

Maximizing the Collective Intelligence of Teams

Unlike individuals, for whom intelligence is very difficult to change, it may be possible for groups of people to effectively increase their collective intelligence. According to research conducted by Dr. Thomas W. Malone and his colleagues at the MIT Center for Collective Intelligence, a group's collective intelligence is correlated with three factors that may help teams essentially work smarter.

First, a group's collective intelligence is significantly correlated with the *average social perceptiveness* of the individual members. Interestingly, however, the average intelligence of the individuals is only weakly correlated. In other words, just because a group consists entirely of smart people does not necessarily mean that that group will have a higher collective intelligence, but groups within which individuals are good at perceiving the emotions and social cues of others stand a greater chance of having a higher collective intelligence.

The second factor is the *evenness of conversational turn taking*. Groups in which one person dominates the conversation are, on average, less intelligent than groups where conversational turn taking is more evenly shared.

Third, the collective intelligence of a group is significantly correlated with the percentage of females in the group; more women means more intelligent groups. According to Malone, this last factor is statistically mediated in large part by the first factor. In other words, it's well established that women generally score higher than men on social sensitivity tests.

To increase the collective intelligence of groups, then, it may be worthwhile to maximize the number of people who are high on social sensitivity, whether these people are male or female, and to encourage equitable conversational turn taking.[9]

Inspire Team Members (Even Before You Meet)

Why wait until the first meeting to develop a sense of camaraderie and trust with team members?

Use your initial communiqués (in person or electronic) to describe the purpose of the team in the context of the broader goals of your organization and the members' value to the team. Underscore the benefits that team members realize from serving on the team, such as learning new skills

TRUST AN

EVERY SU

COLLABO

CHORS

CCESSFUL

RATION.

or showcasing existing ones, gaining visibility and exposure across the company, exploring new career possibilities or being part of an exciting new venture.

Describe how the team will benefit from each prospective team member's specific skills and abilities, such as organizational, subject matter or tools expertise.

Here are three mistakes to avoid during initial conversations with new teams:

- → Steer clear of vague generalizations. ("You always do a great job.")
- → Don't over-emphasize the person's functional or departmental position. ("We need someone from your department.")
- → Don't stress the fact that the person was not a first choice. ("I really hope you'll agree to be on the team. Everyone else says they're too busy.")

If you begin by establishing a positive outlook among the individuals before they even come together, you'll jumpstart the process of building team trust.

Defining Individual Roles and Responsibilities

A shared goal for a cross-functional team is bigger than any one of the functions involved.

Team members must have a clear idea of their individual roles and responsibilities. Without these, it's hard for people to know what is expected of them, and it's easy for them to disengage. Some roles and responsibilities will be determined by the unique purpose and goals of the team, while others are more universal and common across teams.

You can split up roles and responsibilities across multiple people, or you can regularly rotate some of them. Either way, you need to be clear—everyone on the team should know who is responsible for what. Some typical universal roles are described here.

Executive Sponsor. The executive sponsor has the appropriate clout and natural authority to make good decisions.

General responsibilities could include:

- → Ensuring the team's work supports the organization's overall vision and strategies
- → Championing the team
- → Obtaining budgets
- → Accepting responsibility for escalated problems
- → Signing off on documents such as the team charter
- → Removing roadblocks

How to avoid failure: Get involved from the very beginning so the team's charter is aligned with the broader company vision. And remember to share the big picture perspective throughout the project to prevent the team from straying from what's important.

Team Lead. The team lead is an agent and advocate for the executive sponsor and/or the larger organization. The lead is responsible for providing direction to the team and maximizing its success. The lead is expected to use his or her influence to resolve issues and find opportunities for the team. It may make sense to have more than one lead. Team leaders should actively ensure that all members share perspectives, drawing out individuals who might have things to offer that aren't readily apparent.

General responsibilities could include:

- → Serving as representative and advocate for the executive sponsor
- → Ensuring that requirements are properly defined and met

- → Correcting course throughout the life cycle of the team
- → Facilitating and driving team process
- → Defining the decision-making process
- → Reporting progress to the executive sponsor
- → Accounting for the overall success of the team

How to avoid failure: Establish and exercise 51 percent decision-making rights to break logjams that occur on collaborative teams. This is especially important on cross-functional teams that do not have clear paths of escalation. Remember, too, that consensus is the enemy of collaboration. Teams can often quickly reach natural agreement but when members with different points of view resort to consensus building, you lose the value of having diversity. In the spirit of consensus-building, the result is often a compromise that represents the lowest common denominator among the group. Focus on the best decision, not the easiest one.

Creating and maintaining effective teams takes careful planning and systematic monitoring.

Operations Lead. The operations lead is the glue that holds the team together. This role helps the team stay on track by providing structure and process. Some operations leads may have communications responsibilities as well.

General responsibilities could include:

- → Maintaining the overall calendar, agenda and materials
- → Managing logistics (such as scheduling meetings, locations and so on)
- → Tracking action items
- → Creating and distributing meeting minutes
- → Coordinating the creation, use and maintenance of collaborative virtual work spaces
- → Acting as a central point of coordination
- → Assembling and distributing materials

- → Ensuring team decisions and actions are communicated
- → Coordinating interactions with other teams
- → Managing external communications (potentially in partnership with the team lead)
- → Preparing for operational or executive reviews

How to avoid failure: Don't over-emphasize process to the point of stifling the potential value of the team's collective value. Collaboration involves people, and human interactions do not always fit cleanly into a template, format or allotted time on the agenda. Be flexible enough to let ideas and discussion flourish, and adapt the process to fit the characteristics of the team.

Meeting Facilitator. The meeting facilitator ensures that meetings follow the agendas and agreed-upon ground rules for collaboration, and that all attendees have the opportunity to participate.

General responsibilities could include:

- → Overseeing the meeting process and time
- → Bringing attention to conversations that may not support the agenda
- → Intervening when meetings are being dominated by a few participants or when team members seem to have checked out
- → Identifying ground rules that are not being followed

How to avoid failure: This role requires you to step back, keeping one eye on the process and one on the proceedings so the team's overall direction doesn't start to stray from the purpose expressed in the team charter. This is sometimes referred to as the "balcony" role, given its responsibility to keep the big picture in mind.

Team Member. Team members should be chosen for their ability to contribute important information and perspectives during team discussions, align resources to the work of the team, provide subject-matter expertise or to apply skills required to execute on work streams.

EXPERT TIP ON BEHAVIOR

> **"People working in passive-aggressive organizations feel strongly that they don't know which decisions they're responsible for, that no decision is ever final, that good information is hard to obtain, and that the quality of their work is not being accurately appraised. People in resilient organizations feel the opposite."**
>
> —from "The Passive-Aggressive Organization" by Gary L. Nielson, Bruce A. Pasternack and Karen E. Van Nuys, *Harvard Business Review*, October 2005

General responsibilities could include:

- → Actively supporting and driving key team priorities and initiatives inside their functions and, if possible, ensuring functional support of those priorities
- → Executing individual tasks and prioritizing team success over individual or departmental performance
- → Accepting personal responsibility for the success of the team's cross-functional efforts
- → Attending all sessions and bringing energy, passion and commitment to the challenge at hand

How to avoid failure: Team members representing a function, department or business unit on a cross-functional team should take the time to clearly establish with their command chain whether they have the power to speak for that function in terms of budget, head count or other resources during decision-making discussions. This will help them to know when they can act with confidence on behalf of their home department, and when they need to escalate decisions to others.

What Makes a Team Perform Well?

Most members of high-performing teams report that it's fun and satisfying to work on collaborative teams because they are asked to contribute at their highest potential and they learn a lot along the way. Characteristics of high-performing teams include the following:

- → People have solid and deep trust in each other and in the team's purpose—they feel free to express feelings and ideas.
- → Everybody is working toward the same goals.
- → Team members are clear on how to work together and how to accomplish tasks.
- → Everyone understands both team and individual performance goals and knows what is expected.
- → Team members actively diffuse tension and friction in a relaxed and informal atmosphere.
- → The team engages in extensive discussion, and everyone gets a chance to contribute—even the introverts.
- → Disagreement is viewed as a good thing and conflicts are managed. Criticism is constructive and is oriented toward problem solving and removing obstacles.
- → The team makes decisions when there is natural agreement—in the cases where agreement is elusive, a

decision is made by the team lead or executive sponsor, after which little second-guessing occurs.

- → Each team member carries his or her own weight and respects the team processes and other members.
- → The leadership of the team shifts from time to time, as appropriate, to drive results. No individual members are more important than the team.

A team charter paves the way for collaborative success by providing clarity that builds trust and accountability. With a team charter in place, you'll be able to unlock the potential value of your people by empowering them to contribute. In the long run, teams with a clear purpose and good chemistry drive business results. Job satisfaction goes up, employees stay engaged in their work and everybody wins.

60 SECOND WRAP

:00 High-performing teams share a number of characteristics: mutual trust and respect, unity of purpose and well understood processes for managing operations.

:15 As more companies work in cross-functional or virtual teams, the need increases for a consistent framework to encourage trust, accountability and better performance.

:25 Minimizing uncertainty through increased transparency builds trust that is critical to successful collaboration. Clarity and trust breed individual and team accountability.

:35 Creating a team charter gives clarity to a team's purpose, role, shared goals and scope. A team charter should include ground rules for teamwork. A team charter can be created before, after or in tandem with a VSEM (or similar) template.

:50 Teams perform best when you clearly define individual roles and responsibilities. Common roles are:

01 Executive sponsor

02 Team lead

03 Operations lead

04 Meeting facilitator

04 Team member

6

STOP WASTING TIME

Use this framework for collaborative meetings to make the most of your time together.

EXCHANGE

(EXCHANGE BIG IDEAS WITH OTHERS)

(ENGAGE IN A CONVERSATION THAT DRIVES DECISIONS ON SPECIFIC ISSUES)

(INFORM OTHERS OF PROGRESS OR A DIRECTIVE)

EXECUTIVE SUMMARY

Whether participants are spread around a campus or across the globe, collaborative teams are not immune to that dreaded organizational disease, *meetingitis*.

Here's a simple model to make any type of meeting run smoother, end on time and produce results. We've also included some advice for making your virtual meetings more powerful.

"Who called this meeting?"
"Do we have an agenda?"
"Does anyone know why we're meeting?"

How often do you find yourself asking questions like these during a meeting? Increased collaboration means more meetings—whether it's to plan, debate, troubleshoot, share progress or report results. And the frenetic pace of business makes meeting preparation more important than ever. It's a rare meeting that can't be shortened or re-engineered to engage all participants.

The *Clarity of Purpose* model is a best practice we use to establish clear meeting objectives and reduce the time it takes to get people aligned. This model matches meeting *goals* with meeting *formats*; prepares meeting organizers, presenters and participants; and improves the quality of their collaborative efforts.

The advice may sound intuitive, but so often we fail to follow it: Each time you bring a group of people together, it's best to define the meeting's purpose, indicate who's in charge of what and clearly state what a successful outcome looks like. You need to bring the same rigor and discipline that you've applied to the company vision and strategy, as well as the team charter, to every meeting you host.

Here's a straightforward four-step process for running better collaborative meetings.

Step 1: Define the Purpose

Why have you called your meeting? It sounds like an obvious question, but meetings have different purposes (and some have no apparent purpose at all). We've identified nine types of meetings, from a simple informational meeting to a strategic decision-making session. Develop your meeting's framework and agenda by matching it to the type of meeting you want to hold.

Making Strategic Decisions
At the very top of the list is the most important type of meeting, the one designed to help you and your team make a strategic decision that will drive the direction of the company, function or group.

Challenging Thinking
Sometimes you need to call a meeting in order to challenge established thinking by engaging with outside thought leaders, analysts, consultants and customers.

Brainstorming
This kind of session brings people together to get creative ideas flowing.

Correcting Course
Often you need a meeting to use your influence or the influence of others to correct your course or make a strategic adjustment.

Educating and Informing
This common meeting type is used to educate others so that they can align to the company direction and embrace decisions that have already been made.

Inspiring
Every leader must sometimes call meetings to inspire small or large groups, so that they can act on decisions that affect the company direction.

Measuring Progress
Mundane but critical, progress meetings are designed to check status and metrics through an operational review process.

Planning for Execution
The vision sessions are over, the strategies are in place, now it's time to start up the engine. This type of meeting lays out who does what and when.

Consultative Problem Solving
These meetings bring experts and decision makers together to solve a well-defined problem.

Some meetings combine several meeting types; an informational meeting might be followed by a brainstorming session. Treat each section as its own meeting, following the steps in this model.

Step 2: Establish Presentation Goals and Structure

Will your meeting involve a number of interactions or just a few? Do you have lots of information to impart or not much at all? Are you looking for agreement or explaining a decision?

At the heart of the Clarity of Purpose Model, Step 2 revolves around three meeting formats: *Exchange, Engage* and *Inform*. When you establish presentation goals and structure, all participants can understand their roles.

An *exchange* meeting involves sharing big ideas with participating attendees. You'll need to dedicate a larger percentage of meeting time for discussions and relatively less time for formal presentations.

Use the exchange format to brainstorm solutions when your team has to resolve problems or come to agreement on open issues or strategy decisions. Use the time allotted for formal presentation to communicate the structure or parameters for the exchange. Perhaps team members need to take opposing sides of an issue and debate, or consider and prioritize a set of potential strategy options. The parameters of the exchange session should be determined prior to the meeting. Brainstorming is much more productive when it's structured rather than open-ended.

***Exchange* big ideas with attendees to resolve issues or reach agreement.**

An *engage* meeting is one in which everyone has already agreed to the big ideas and now you need to have a dialogue around strategy. Because you don't have to schedule time for a deep exchange, you may be able to get by with a slightly shorter meeting time. Typical examples of engage meetings include discussions around operational requirements, resource alignment and business impact. In an engage meeting, presenters want to come into the conversation with a strategy and walk out with the agreement or decision needed to move forward.

***Engage* in a conversation that drives decisions on specific issues.**

Meetings using the *inform* format take place when the

MEETING FORMATS

EXCHANGE, ENGAGE OR INFORM?

TEST YOURSELF

WHAT'S THE TYPE?

A. Exchange B. Engage or C. Inform

Q: Everyone (or most people) in the meeting already knows and has agreed to the vision and strategy. Now it's time to review flight plans.

A: ....

Q: We want to drive a discussion that maximizes all the skills, talents and perspectives in the meeting.

A: ....

Q: Everyone (or most people) in the meeting already know the vision/direction, and now the group needs to figure out how to get there.

A: ....

Answers: 1.c; 2.a; 3.b

MEETING FORMAT

EXCHANGE

TIME → UP TO 2 HOURS

25% PRESENTATION 75% DISCUSSION

NO. OF PEOPLE → >15

DESCRIPTION

The group is trying to agree on a vision, future direction or a very big and complex cross-functional goal

Discussion leverages all the skills, talents and perspectives in the room

The presenter drives a brainstorm, debate or discussion to help the team come to agreement

ADJUSTMENTS FOR VIRTUAL MEETINGS

Assign roles, especially a web collaboration monitor

Set up panels for video and chat features

If you're using a web-sharing collaboration solution, use the application's whiteboard feature to allow remote attendees to see the whiteboard or projector in the conference room

Share a document so all attendees can edit or at least use annotation tools

If one person is editing, share the document so all attendees can see what is being edited

Include interactive elements at least every 5–10 minutes to avoid losing the remote attendees

MEETING FORMAT

ENGAGE

TIME → UP TO 1 HOUR

50% PRESENTATION | 50% DISCUSSION

NO. OF PEOPLE → >20

DESCRIPTION

Everyone or almost everyone already knows the team's vision/direction and now needs to figure out how to get there

The presenters come in with a strategy and hope to leave with a consensus/agreement/compromise to move the team forward

The group expects to make one or more decisions

ADJUSTMENTS FOR VIRTUAL MEETINGS

Assign roles, especially a web collaboration monitor

Set up panels for video and chat features

If you're using a web-sharing collaboration solution, use the application's whiteboard feature to allow remote attendees to see the whiteboard or projector in the conference room

Share a document so all attendees can edit or at least use annotation tools

If one person is editing, share the document so all attendees can see what is being edited

MEETING FORMAT

INFORM

TIME → UP TO 30 MINS

75% PRESENTATION | 25% DISCUSSION

NO. OF PEOPLE → many

DESCRIPTION

Everyone or almost everyone already knows and has agreed to the team's vision and strategy

It serves as an update on execution

Its purpose is to keep the stakeholders abreast of progress and address issues that surface along the way, or to educate people on some topic

It does not require a decision to be made

ADJUSTMENTS FOR VIRTUAL MEETINGS

Without interaction, keep inform sessions to approximately 15 minutes

During Q&A, make sure to solicit input from remote attendees

MATCHING MEETING TYPES WITH SUGGESTED FORMATS

MEETING TYPE	PURPOSE	SUGGESTED FORMAT
Make Strategic Decisions	Make a strategic decision that will drive the direction of the company, function or group	**Exchange**
Challenge Thinking	Challenge thinking by engaging with external thought leaders and customers	**Engage**
Course Correct	Use inside or outside influence and/or knowledge to correct course	**Engage**
Educate/ Inform	Educate groups and individuals so that they can align to the decisions and the company direction	**Inform**
Inspire	Inspire large groups so that they can act on decisions and the company direction	**Engage** or **Inform**
Measure Progress	Check status and metrics through an operational review process	**Inform**
Plan	Plan for execution	**Engage**
Brainstorm	Brainstorm and categorize ideas	**Exchange**
Consultative Problem Solving	Work together to solve a problem (the team can have equal knowledge of the issues or consult subject-matter experts)	**Exchange**

big ideas have been agreed upon, the strategy is in place and you're updating everyone on progress or addressing issues that have surfaced along the way. Ideally, this should be the briefest of all meetings because you don't have to schedule time to exchange ideas or engage in a dialogue (though, of course, you'll want to leave time for questions and answers).

Step 3: Clearly Communicate Expectations

Next it's time to clearly communicate expectations to presenters and participants in the meeting. Use the one-page speaker brief to establish the goal, format and desired areas of content for each presentation.

This structure guides the meeting without being too prescriptive. Send this brief to each speaker and check in with him or her to ensure that roles and responsibilities are clear. Set clear expectations about what will be covered in the meeting, paying special attention to removing agenda items that don't add value to the discussion.

Inform attendees of progress or a directive.

The brief should indicate if the meeting you are conducting will be an *exchange*-, an *engage*- or an *inform*-type meeting. It lets the speakers know how much time they have and the key discussion points they should cover.

You will have certain topics you want presenters to articulate. Naturally, they will also want to bring ideas. If you're clear about your expectations, presenters will be more prepared, and the meeting will run more smoothly.

Step 4: Own Your Meeting

Take responsibility for the success of your meeting before it happens, during the meeting and afterward. It takes time and energy, but imagine how everyone will feel after you have mastered one of the rarest of all organizational accomplishments: a productive meeting that ends on time.

The formula for great meetings is really quite simple. It just requires a little bit of planning. Define the purpose of your meeting, establish the goals and structure, clearly communicate expectations and own it.

EXPERT TIP ON THE IMPORTANCE OF TIME

"Probably the single most damaging shortage that most teams suffer from is time. If you're going to bring a team together, they ought to be making important decisions, and if they're going to be making important decisions, then they really need the time to have the robust debate and get the issues on the table that need to be discussed."

—from *Senior Leadership Teams* by Ruth Wageman, Debra A. Nunes, James A. Burress and J. Richard Hackman, Harvard Business Press, 2007

Tips for Having Great Virtual Meetings

New technology and the reality of working in global organizations means we are replacing traditional in-person meetings with travel-free, technology-enabled, face-to-face collaboration that can occur at anytime, with anyone, anywhere in the world.

The virtual workplace has many advantages, but it also introduces new challenges. We work with people we've never met before, and we cannot bond in the same way we do when we are sitting across the table from them.

The three most important ingredients of a successful virtual meeting are *trust, communication* and *ready access to information*. Here are a few tips to help you succeed:

- → Before the meeting, make sure attendees have all the preparation materials they will need and the time to review them.
- → Begin with a quick warm-up. For example, start the meeting by asking remote attendees to describe what's happening in their country, town or office.
- → During "blended" meetings, where some attendees are gathering in person and others are participating virtually, address remote attendees first and then offer the opportunity to speak to in-person attendees.
- → Identify in-person attendees. In-room speakers—whether presenting or making a comment—should introduce themselves so that remote attendees know who is speaking.
- → Ask remote attendees to be vocal. Emphasize that it is their responsibility to let in-person people know if they cannot hear or follow the discussion.
- → Don't assume everyone is comfortable with the virtual collaboration technology. Communicate and publish the location and guidelines for the tools you're using.

A virtual meeting can be a great thing, but it's never a sure thing.

- → Rotate meeting times. Ensure that each time zone has a meeting scheduled during normal business hours.
- → Solicit participation. Regularly ask remote attendees if they have comments and encourage participants to post a message.
- → Assign a meeting monitor. Keep an eye out for questions, IMs or chat postings and interjects from remote attendees.
- → If your virtual team includes customers, partners, suppliers or vendors, ensure the security of your documents and corporate information.
- → Avoid colloquialisms, acronyms and corporate-speak if you have nonnative speakers.

→ Wrap up by documenting key discussion points, decisions and action items.

EXPERT TIP ON SKILLS FOR THE VIRTUAL AGE

"The masterful virtual presenter possesses two demonstrable skill sets. First is the skill to create and communicate clear, concise, credible and compelling presentations to a dispersed and mostly unseen audience, and second is the ability to keep his or her audience members as attentive and engaged as if they were all in the same room with the presenter."

—Brad Holst, Mandel Communications

Use Vocal Energy to Engage Your Webcast Audience
Leaders are often called on to lead virtual presentations, often before hundreds of online participants. The transition to virtual is not a natural one for most presenters and a presenter's lack of virtual communication skills becomes evident almost immediately. Even great ideas can get lost in a faceless drone, and audience attention spans can quickly evaporate.

When you're face-to-face, more than 80 percent of your audience impact comes from the visual cues that you give off as you speak. In a non-visual webcast, more than 80 percent of your impact will come from *your voice alone*. Presenting in a virtual format requires you to channel your energy to an audience that you can't see and that can't see you. Here are some helpful tips for virtual presentation success:

- *Speak with conviction.* Let your natural energy and passion come through by varying the volume, tone and pace of your voice to add authority, interest and emphasis to your content.
- *Don't race.* Many webcast presenters sound like they are in a mad rush to get their content out. Slow it down. After you emphasize a key point or bring up a new slide, pause to take a breath, give yourself a moment to think, and allow the audience to process your information.
- *Be in command of your body.* Stand or sit forward in an engaged posture with your weight balanced and your feet flat on the floor. Body posture and movement influence both vocal projection and inflection. The more you involve your hands, arms and body, the more energized and confident your voice will sound.
- *Turn off instant messaging, auto email notifications and calendar reminders.* This is vitally important. You'd be surprised just how much a pop-up can distract a webcast speaker, even if the audience can't see it. And if you happen to be sharing your desktop with your audience, it can potentially be embarrassing.
- *Clean up your computer desktop.* If you plan on sharing your desktop with your audience, think about what a sloppy, disorganized-looking desktop may say about you. Make sure your desktop doesn't contain anything that might be offensive to your audience or make an impression that you don't want your audience members to have.

60 SECOND WRAP

:00 Increased collaboration means more meetings, making it even more important to ensure that meeting time is highly productive.

:20 The Clarity of Purpose Model is a great way to set and attain meeting objectives.

01 In an *exchange* meeting, you share big ideas with the participants.

02 In an *engage* meeting, everyone has already agreed to the big ideas and now you need to have a dialogue around strategy.

03 In an *inform* meeting, everyone gets progress updates or addresses issues that have surfaced along the way, after major decisions have been made.

:30 Know your meeting types and plan accordingly.

01 Making Strategic Decisions: Establishing top-level direction

02 Challenging Thinking: Engaging with others

03 Correcting Course: Using influence to make a needed strategic adjustment

04 Educating and Informing: Telling people what they need to know so they can align with company direction

05 Inspiring: Motivating groups to act

06 Measuring Progress: Checking status on goals

07 Planning for Execution: Laying out who does what and when

08 Brainstorming: Getting the creative ideas flowing

09 Consultative Problem Solving: Solving a well-defined problem

:50 The new collaboration experience enables us to form virtual teams of talented individuals, regardless of where they are located. With effective management, you can turn these virtual teams into a powerful asset for your organization. Virtual meetings require some extra work on your part to keep remote attendees engaged. It's worth the extra effort.

7

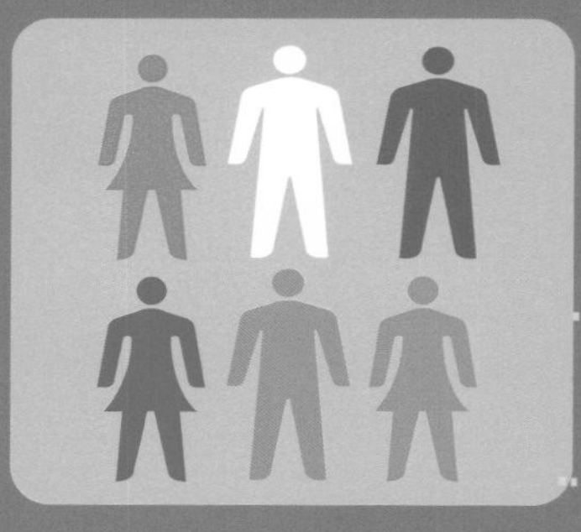

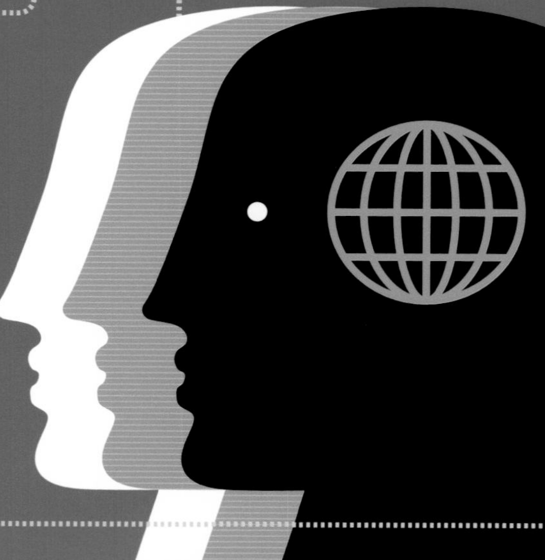

UNLOCK THE COLLABORATION TOOLBOX

Support your collaboration strategy with the right technology solutions.

FOUR COLLABORATION TRENDS

MOBILE
SOCIAL
VISUAL
VIRTUAL

SHAPE HOW WE WORK

EXECUTIVE SUMMARY

Four important trends shape the collaboration technology toolbox: mobile, social, visual and virtual. Together, they represent a fundamental shift in the way we interact with colleagues as well as customers, partners and suppliers.

Think about how these technologies factor into your business strategy. Then assemble the right collaboration portfolio to help your organization be more agile and meet your business objectives faster.

Ever-advancing information technology has paved the way for new business models and altered the competitive landscape for good. As you navigate this fundamental shift, the collaboration technology portfolio, married with culture and process transformation, provides an answer to the challenges that lie ahead. Your customers, partners and competitors are changing the way they communicate—from a traditional document- and audio-centric approach to an increasingly video-rich and interactive one.

It's up to you to assemble the right tools into an integrated portfolio that brings people together faster and helps them interact with more agility. Your tools should reflect the four major technology trends that are changing how we work: *mobile, social, visual* and *virtual*. Let's take a look at each one.

→ **Mobile**

By 2013, mobile phones will overtake PCs as the most common method of accessing the Internet, according to predictions from Gartner.[10] Meanwhile, the proliferation of smart phones has outpaced our wildest expectations. Expect mobile applications to be a critical component for your collaboration strategy moving forward.

→ **Social**

Facebook and other social media platforms are driving new behaviors, changing the way people interact. We're seeing powerful benefits—and some interesting challenges—as the trend makes its way into business. Social media isn't a fad. It's a fundamental shift in the way we communicate.

→ **Visual**

Look around and you'll see video solutions popping up everywhere, from the boardroom to the desktop to the hotel room and on all sorts of mobile devices. Rich media experiences in our daily work environment collapse time and space, so colleagues that are oceans apart feel as though they are meeting face-to-face. By facilitating authentic communication and lifelike interactions, video builds trust, increases accountability and enhances the act of collaborating. Document-centric communication has gone the way of the inter-office envelope, and pervasive video is the new voice.

All forms of video generated approximately 51 percent of consumer Internet traffic in 2010. By 2013, that percentage is expected to surpass 90 percent.[11]

→ **Virtual**

The virtual experience provides more flexibility. Employees can work on any application or access any content, using any device from any location. Companies can host applications on-site or in the cloud. Virtualization technology enables this remote work experience by making the delivery of collaboration applications transparent to the user. Virtualization technology promises to redefine what we think of as "the desktop." If you aren't investigating the cost and service delivery implications of going virtual, start now.

CASE STUDY

Architectural Firm Kohn Pedersen Fox Takes Collaboration to New Heights

From New Songdo City in South Korea and the Abu Dhabi International Airport, to the Shanghai World Financial Center and the master plan for New York City's Hudson Yards, architectural firm Kohn Pedersen Fox Associates (KPF) designs some of the most recognizable buildings and well-traveled spaces in the world. Its projects comprise millions of square feet and impact many different cultures. While the firm encourages individual creativity, collaboration both internally among the firm's global offices and externally with clients and project teams is essential for exchanging information, sharing expertise and making faster and more informed decisions.

The prospect of travel is a constant for the project teams in this global organization of 550 people. However, a holistic collaboration strategy, centered around the pervasive use of video and web conferencing, has transformed the company's operating model. Through collaborative working sessions and client meetings, KPF executes complex design projects across geographically dispersed teams, while reducing the costs and inconveniences of travel.

By leveraging the time zones of their globally diverse staff, KPF's architectural teams are able to extend the normal work day by overlapping team efforts in multiple offices—collaboration can take place 24 hours a day. Telepresence, video conferencing and video phones connected through their global network infrastructure make every team and client interaction feel local and personal, while a unified communications platform enables complete mobility and lowers telephony costs. With video as a fundamental aspect of its collaboration approach, KPF can present itself to clients as a local company, no matter where the next opportunity arises.

Collaboration in a Post-PC Era

The once-dominant desktop PC model has exploded into a multitude of technology choices that empower employees to interact and work together in new ways. This is the dawn of the anytime, anywhere workplace, fueled by networked devices using open standards. It's a dramatic shift for employees and companies that reflects several major changes in the traditional PC landscape:

→ **Applications**
Blend familiar business applications like email with new social applications and you bring people, communities and information together in entirely new ways. The old software provisioning model is moving toward an app store model where users can serve themselves. Think iTunes, which has exceeded 15 billion downloads. But how does the app store concept work in the enterprise, and how do we ensure security and policy control?

→ **Operating Systems**
Five years ago, Microsoft Windows powered nearly every computing device. Today, possibilities abound as Mac OS, iOS Android and others have entered the market. The pace of this transition is incredible. There are 550,000 Android activations every day, and no one can predict which new operating system will emerge tomorrow.[12] All of this gives businesses and their employees more choices about how they use technology to interact with others. But the need to support multiple operating systems can impede collaboration efforts.

→ **Devices**
The desktop PC and laptop have plenty of company in the marketplace today. More than 3.6 billion mobile devices, including smart phones, tablets, thin clients and video devices, are connected to the network.[13] As more employees bring their preferred gadgets to work so they can work in the way they feel makes them the most productive, IT must integrate and secure them within the context of the enterprise network.

→ **Deployment Options**

Traditional technology architectures have evolved significantly in recent years from centralized data centers to virtualized data centers, and the cloud is now an increasingly compelling option for business applications, offering companies more flexibility and driving down costs. Meanwhile, desktop virtualization has benefits in terms of cost and data security. The challenge from a collaboration point of view is ensuring that real-time voice and video work well in a virtualized and secure environment.

Cloud Computing Defined

Cloud computing enables services and content to be dynamically delivered on demand—on a massive scale and with high efficiency. This rapidly emerging computing option gives companies the ability to deliver more interactive and more rapidly available services and content to employees as well as customers at dramatically lower cost.

Together, these changes represent a shift into a Post-PC era—one that is reshaping collaboration in dramatic ways:

- An individual's sphere of influence expands from a few to many people
- Communities change from hierarchical to self-organizing models
- Content evolves from document- and voice-centric to rich media and video
- Information moves from something you search for to something that finds you
- Security moves from a focus strictly inside the firewall to one that extends to customers, partners and suppliers

COLLABORATION THEN AND NOW

The new era of anytime, anywhere collaboration means that leaders have to evolve how they think about people, communities and content in the collaborative workplace.

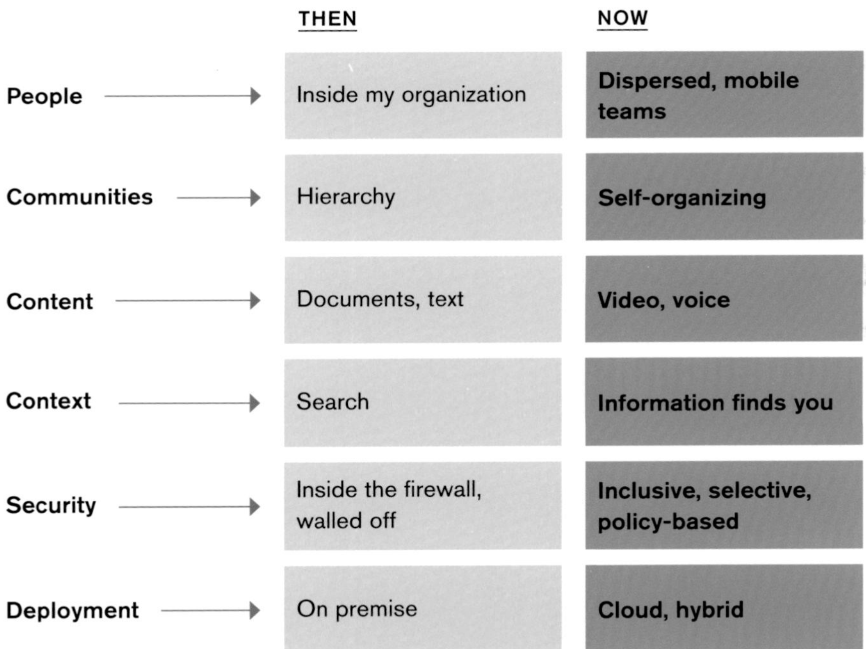

THEN
NOW
People
Inside my organization
Dispersed, mobile teams
Communities
Hierarchy
Self-organizing
Content
Documents, text
Video, voice
Context
Search
Information finds you
Security
Inside the firewall, walled off
Inclusive, selective, policy-based
Deployment
On premise
Cloud, hybrid

The Collaboration Portfolio

To capitalize on the power of collaboration, you need a broad portfolio of technologies that work seamlessly together. They should support your company's specific business processes and the ways in which your people interact. The end goal is an integrated and natural collaboration experience for end users, whether they are employees in a bank, customers in a store, forklift operators on the manufacturing floor or law-enforcement officers keeping our communities safe.

When considered as part of a holistic strategy, collaboration tools improve communication within and beyond your company walls.

Seven solutions make up the collaboration portfolio:

→ Internet Protocol (IP) Communications
→ Mobile Applications
→ Telepresence and Video
→ Conferencing
→ Messaging
→ Enterprise Social Software
→ Customer Care

ELEMENTS OF THE COLLABORATION TECHNOLOGY PORTFOLIO

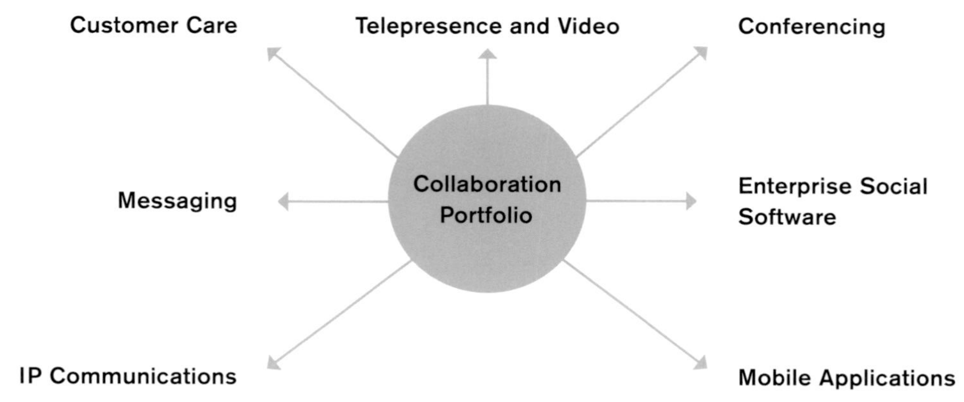

IP Communications: Build a Strong Foundation

The starting point for most collaboration strategies is voice communication services. This includes IP Communications, which is made up of IP telephony, communications endpoints and applications. Deploying IP Communications used to mean connecting one physical—or hard—device, such as an office phone, for each employee on the network. Today, the number of devices per employee has multiplied, with numerous soft phone clients and mobile devices in the mix.

Based on the universal, open standard of networking, IP Communications technology provides reliable and advanced communication capabilities for your staff, no matter where they work. It allows you to manage voice, video, mobility and telepresence services between different endpoints, mobile devices and multimedia applications so that people can move fluidly from a land-line call to a web conference to a mobile device. Meetings can support a mix of communication technologies. Some participants will join on video, while others dial in from land lines and still others connect using mobile phones. In this way, you eliminate communication silos and ensure a seamless communication experience that's flexible enough to accommodate each individual, wherever they happen to be at the time the meeting starts. In the end, technology costs go down, while productivity driven by improved collaboration goes up.

Mobile Applications: Stay Connected on the Go

Up to 90 percent of employees work outside of corporate headquarters today. And by 2012, some 30 percent of the global workforce will be mobile workers.[14] In a mobile world, your physical location becomes irrelevant. Your workspace must go where you go, and give you the same set of tools, content and collaborative capabilities as you have when you're sitting at your desk.

Mobile applications are a critical piece of the puzzle because they let employees connect, communicate and collaborate regardless of where they are. Examples include mobile applications and meeting applications for smart phones, business tablets and wireless IP phones. When IT departments have a clear policy for managing mobile communications, they can increase employee productivity while controlling costs like roaming charges. Remember, decisions you make about mobile devices today affect the collaboration strategy for your organization tomorrow.

CASE STUDY

Nottingham University Hospitals Redefines Nursing with Mobile Applications

With more than 13,000 staff working across two main campuses, and providing care to more than 2.5 million people, Nottingham University Hospitals NHS Trust (NUH) is one of the UK's largest providers of health care. Spread across 90 acres, the city hospital campus to the North of Nottingham is believed to be the largest health facility in Europe. In a workplace this large, it has been extremely difficult for doctors and nurses to collaborate. Simply finding people when you needed them posed a serious and time-consuming challenge.

Until recently, when a doctor or nurse needed a senior opinion from a clinician, they used a fixed phone to call an operator to page that person. Then they waited, and waited, for the recipient to receive the page, finish whatever he or she was doing, find a phone and return the call. Clinicians were constantly interrupted, precious time was lost and care givers ran the risk of failing to delivering the best care.

Communication in the emergency department was especially difficult. Messages were broadcast over a sound system, creating a constant chatter heard by all—doctors, nurses, patients and visitors. Yet, there was no guarantee the right person would answer the call. On a busy shift, the senior doctor might get paged 10 or 12 times an hour.

Enter mobile communications. With a unified communications system, clinicians engage in anywhere, anytime collaboration using integrated wireless and messaging technologies. Instead of pagers, clinicians carry wireless IP phones and can reach each other directly using directory-based dialing; video capabilities allow doctors in different facilities to meet face-to-face without the need to travel.

With all information exchanged over a single platform, clinicians no longer walk a mile to a ward and discover the job was done by someone else. Patients no longer sit in the waiting room after an x-ray until a staff member notices they need to be brought back to the emergency department. Instead, the department is alerted when a patient is ready for transfer.

Better collaboration also helped the hospital improve clinical safety by lowering the chance of vital instructions for patient care falling through the cracks. In the inevitable on-the-go communication that happens in these wards, staff might overlook—or simply run out of time to attend to—a task that's communicated verbally or written on a slip of paper. Now, those requests are recorded on the wireless device, improving efficiency, accountability, training and, ultimately, the quality of care.

Better staff collaboration has delivered considerably shorter patient wait times, which means NUH can treat more patients. In fact, NUH eliminated about 40 minutes of patient waiting time per shift for every doctor. In gynecology surgery, turnaround time for patients fell from 45 minutes to just five. The solution also offers visibility into staffing needs. With increased efficiency and predictability, NUH can clearly see how many clinicians are needed to handle the workload on a given shift. All of these improvements add up to a satisfied staff that provides better patient care, and the hospital expects to recoup its collaboration investment in 13 months.

Telepresence: Lifelike Video Conferencing

The need to collaborate across time and space is urgent, but opportunities for team building through face-to-face interaction are more and more rare. Telepresence systems close this

HOW WIL
COLLABO
THE POST

YOU
RATE IN
-PC ERA?

If the majority of human communication is non-verbal, how much information are you missing during audio-only conferences?

gap with high-definition video, life-size images and realistic lighting and sound.

Unlike the standard video-conferencing experience, where participants are keenly aware that they are participating remotely, telepresence is so immersive that participants forget about the technology interface and focus instead on their interactions with others. As a result, they can hold highly productive virtual sessions that bring together talent, resources and decision makers spread across different regions and business units.

Whether it's an executive review meeting, an engineering workshop or a customer interaction, immersive video helps to build trust quickly to facilitate collaboration.

CASE STUDY

General Electric's Virtual Collaboration Spaces

General Electric (GE) was an early adopter of telepresence for its global executive meetings, but leaders within the company wanted more from the technology than the ability to give executives face time for one-hour review sessions. They wanted to accelerate innovation for products made by engineers in the United States and Europe and sold to markets in China and India. GE entertained a bold concept: Could telepresence imitate the feel of a real working room, where groups of people come together for several hours at a time to solve problems? The challenge was how to capture images of people who are walking around the room, drawing on whiteboards and needing to make eye contact with an audience that's both in the room and virtual.

The solution, a first-of-its-kind Virtual Collaboration Space that takes immersive video conferencing to a whole new level, includes:

→ A telepresence system with voice-activated cameras that follow a speaker around the room

- → Smartboards for electronic whiteboarding
- → An online meeting capability for communicating with people who are not in one of the telepresence rooms
- → Custom-designed collaboration furniture to create a highly interactive environment

With 62 Virtual Collaboration Spaces in use at the time of this writing, and eight expected by the end of 2011, the technology has transformed collaboration at GE. Instead of flying 50 employees to one destination for intensive full-day working sessions, the company can invite participants to a series of virtual sessions. Meeting style, length and frequency can be adjusted to suit the task at hand.

"Virtual Collaboration Spaces are changing the way we work," says GE Chief Technology Officer Greg Simpson. "We might have four teams in four locations working on a problem. The teams listen to comments in breakout sessions and pull in subject-matter experts on the fly. None of this was possible before." Without the need to travel, GE has the luxury of spreading meetings out over a longer period of time, and yet its teams still get the job done faster. The return on investment is all about better decisions, stronger teams and reduced cycle time.

Conferencing: An Integrated Meeting Experience

In business, decisions often require instant input from many places. By itself, the audio conference call often falls short. Conferencing solutions with integrated video, audio and web capabilities make everyday meetings more productive. Participants can deliver presentations, and share documents and applications all within one environment. They can control a remote desktop or pass control to let someone else present.

Actively draw remote attendees into the conversation and discourage multitasking to make virtual meetings as valuable as possible.

Voice identification features indicate who is speaking at any given moment. And recording a meeting is as easy as clicking a mouse.

The Millennial generation has grown up in a networked world and expects to use social media at work. Do you know when Millennials will make up the majority of your workforce?

These virtual conferencing tools facilitate more natural and productive group communication. Meetings run smoother when all participants can see the same presentation, respond to polls and raise their hands to ask a question. It's the difference between an engaged audience that can make collaborative decisions and one that multitasks instead.

Messaging: Communicate Through the Best Channel

When a problem arises in your business, how do you find colleagues to help, and what is the best way to reach them? Enterprise instant messaging products help you locate people and initiate contact through the best medium for the moment, whether it's email, voice messaging, instant messaging or a video phone call. Messaging technology drives productivity and accelerates business by allowing employees to access and deliver messages via any medium, anywhere, on any device.

The messaging category includes voice and unified messaging, enterprise instant messaging, email and presence. Customizable options help you manage calls and voice messages to suit your needs. With messaging, you can choose the best possible communication channel for the circumstances and drive collaboration to a new level.

Enterprise Social Software: The Rise of Social Networking in Business

How many emails are waiting in your inbox right now? And how long does it take to locate a piece of information that someone has sent? We've all been there. Enterprise social software turns time-consuming information hunting into productive dialogues that solve problems.

According to IDC, 57 percent of workers use social media

for business purposes at least once a week.[15] Maybe you've met the type: They read and write blog posts, comment on forums, consult wikis, join communities, share videos and rank and tag information. Well connected and informed, they have their finger on the pulse. They quickly find the information and expertise they need, at the precise moment they need it. They have the ability to make rapid-fire decisions, often involving people outside their own organization. Knowledge seems to flow directly to them; rarely do they need to seek it out. These early adopters have tapped into a powerful resource, and the rest of us aren't far behind.

Enterprise social software creates powerful collaboration networks that extend your sphere of influence way beyond the well-traveled path between your desk and the closest water cooler. In this new model of communication, silos disappear. Teams become dynamic and fluid, disbanding and re-forming as often as new projects require.

Powered by enterprise social software, collaboration networks are to the enterprise what social networks are to consumers.

With enterprise social software and extensive use of video, you increase collaboration and drive global productivity by connecting the right people, information and expertise through virtual workgroups and communities.

Social Conversations Deliver Fast Answers at Cisco

Here at Cisco, we saw an opportunity to help employees manage vast amounts of information with enterprise social software. Our goals were four-fold:

- → Connect the right people, resources and content at the right time
- → Improve communication
- → Facilitate collaboration internally and externally
- → Help our employees learn from one another

In 2010, we launched an initiative called the Integrated Workforce Experience (IWE), a community-building platform that extends collaboration to all employees in a social media context. It's a decisive move away from the old model of publishing static information to web pages on a corporate intranet site.

Today, our employees watch videos, post comments, write blogs and get support all within one environment. Colleagues can find experts, follow people and click to connect and communicate in real time. To date, the platform has been deployed to more than 100,000 Cisco employees and contractors across 165 countries.

Integral to IWE are a growing number of collaborative communities created around job and organizational functions, roles and topics of interest. Cisco teams have formed communities around everything from Selling Cloud to the Amsterdam Green team.

One of those communities, the Global Platform for Sales community, shows the power and flexibility of IWE. Here, the company's worldwide sales team of 17,000 shares best practices, information and tools with cross-functional sales teams across the globe.

Before IWE, when a sales person needed to find an expert in telecommunications or the latest information on our cloud solutions for a customer, he or she might spend days making phone calls, trying to get on calendars, sending emails and searching the company directory. It was a hit-or-miss situation.

Social software has transformed that process. Now a sales person searches for information on *cloud computing* and a Selling Cloud community appears, containing a library of documents, discussion forums, upcoming events and more. If the information isn't available, the sales person can post a comment, tag and share it, and any number of people might respond.

With IWE, Cisco employees can access current information and find experts in a given field, grow their networks and eliminate the need to dig through old material. Our employees are collaborating more naturally, making smarter decisions and accelerating cycle times.

Customer Care: Social CRM

Customer intimacy takes on a whole new meaning in the context of social software. Companies that use collaboration technology for customer care break away from the reactive mode of traditional call centers and set a new standard for customer service. Satisfaction and loyalty improve when you connect customers with the information, expertise and the support they need in their preferred mode of communication.

Customer care tools include contact center routing and queuing, voice self-service and social media customer care. Social media monitoring tools help you track and analyze the conversations that matter to your business. Use these collaboration tools to better meet customer needs and keep a close watch on what customers are saying about you—good or bad.

You can also use these tools to route customers to skilled experts in the contact center or other part of the company to address their needs. Being proactive in this way helps your company enhance service levels, improve loyalty and win new customers, all while protecting your brand.

Can your front-line service representatives connect customers with subject-matter experts in real time? How would customer satisfaction change if they could?

Q&A

The Power of Enterprise 2.0 Technologies

If your competition became three times more productive and you didn't, how worried would you be? This is the question Dr. Andrew McAfee poses when discussing the importance of collaboration. Author of *Enterprise 2.0,* McAfee sees great potential for a more open way of communicating in the workplace. Here he offers leaders words of advice for how to move their organization in this direction.

Q: You coined the term "Enterprise 2.0". Can you describe what you mean?

A: At first, I was skeptical of the whole "Web 2.0" movement. But when I started to look at Wikipedia and Facebook and more recently at things like Twitter and Foursquare, I realized they were all about putting people in touch with each other. Despite their seemingly chaotic nature, these solutions had massive implications for companies across every industry. "Enterprise 2.0" describes the impact these technologies are having on business.

There are three similarities across the Enterprise 2.0 landscape. The first is that these technologies are all public. If you're a knowledge worker, Gen-X or older, you sit in your office, put your head down, do your thinking and communicate with a few other people via point-to-point technologies like email. The only people who know the contents of the email are you and the recipients. When you're done, you distribute the finished product to whoever needs it.

With Enterprise 2.0 tools, you think, work and interact more openly, which seems weird at first. But the more you do it, the more natural it becomes.

The second thing these tools have in common is that they do not dictate terms to users. Unlike an ERP system, for example, Enterprise 2.0 tools impose as few conditions as possible on people, workflows and interactions. You create a digital environment where people can participate at will. These technologies don't care what your job title is or where you sit on the org chart. That encourages a different kind of energy.

It may sound like a recipe for chaos, but patterns tend to emerge over time. And that's the third trait that these tools have in common. People settle into roles, these environments become easy to navigate and something like a workflow appears. The collective intelligence of the organization increases as time goes on.

Q: What advice would you give to help companies see the value of being more open to the Enterprise 2.0 universe?

A: If you want to do what Nelson Mandela talks about—which is to find everyone's "spark of genius" in the organization—you need to give up control and get out of the way. Only then can you harvest the good stuff that emerges.

It's normal to imagine all the bad things that might happen if you let people come together and do whatever they want. But I'm astonished at how rarely any of this happens. In enterprise environments, we see people behaving with a high level of professionalism.

Q: How does an organization make the shift to this way of working?

A: The transition cannot be entirely a bottom-up initiative. It requires a top-down approach in which the formal and informal leaders signal via their actions that they honestly do want this new style of collaboration to happen, and they are going to do what it takes to make it succeed. It can't be lip service. Management needs to send those signals loudly, clearly and often.

That means using the technologies yourself. Maintain a profile on a social network. Start blogging. Get yourself out there in video chats. And don't hand these activities off strictly to your PR staff because people can sniff that out very easily. Authenticity is really important.

You should also take advantage of all the other tools we have in the managerial toolkit: rewards and recognition, status and incentives, performance reviews. All these steps move an organization in the right direction.

Q: Is there an imperative for companies to embrace more collaborative technologies?

A: The imperative is competition. The world is not a sleepy place. Companies are vying with each other for every slice of customer attention and every dollar of revenue. These technologies help solve that age-old challenge articulated by Lew Platt, the former CEO of HP: "If only HP knew what HP knows, we'd be three times as productive." An organization that solves that challenge and becomes three times more productive is sure to win.

Collaboration Without Boundaries: Benefits of an Integrated Portfolio

Before you decide which technologies belong in your collaboration toolbox, consider this: Collaboration is a bit like building a Ferrari. Greatness depends not only on the individual parts but also on the way they are assembled.

If you want an integrated experience for all your employees—regardless of their role, location and points of connection—recognize that decisions you make about mobile devices affect how you'll deploy video, and vice versa. An open, interoperable infrastructure is critical because it gives you flexibility to bring in new technologies as they emerge in the future.

The goal is collaboration without boundaries. Forget work/life balance. This is about work/life integration. You want people working together:

- → Anywhere—at home, the boardroom, the office, a hotel or a soccer game
- → On any device—supporting the end points and platforms that people use today, including PCs, phones and video-enabled mobile devices such as iPads and other tablets
- → Using any content—connecting to any media, whether it's data, voice or video, in the applications that people work in today
- → With the control, policy and flexibility that IT requires

Best of all, there is a powerful network effect to this technology: The more pervasive collaboration becomes, the more powerful its impact. As people start using these tools, they become more productive almost immediately. This new way of working has an addictive quality. Once you get used to the integrated web-conference experience, for example, it seems old fashioned if you have to revert to a phone call where you can't tell who's speaking or collectively work on a shared document in real time.

Start small, at a business-unit level, for example, and you'll quickly see the potential of having the entire organization, as well as customers and partners, on a common platform. Once you see the value and understand the return, you can plot a course to the next level of collaboration.

60 SECOND WRAP

:00 Four technology trends shape the collaboration toolkit—mobile, social, visual and virtual.

:15 The integrated collaboration portfolio consists of seven technologies:

01 IP Communications

02 Mobile applications

03 Telepresence and video

04 Conferencing

05 Messaging

06 Enterprise social software

07 Customer care

:35 Video offers a way to accelerate product development, scale expertise across the company and better integrate global teams.

:40 Mobile technology facilitates the anywhere, anytime workplace.

:45 Social networks and social media help teams find expertise and information faster.

:50 Collaboration without boundaries is the end goal. The technology choices you make today should reflect the collaboration strategy you want to pursue for the future.

8

EIGHT HIGH-IMPACT COLLABORATION OPPORTUNITIES

Identify common business activities that are ripe for transformation.

PRIORITIES

(IDENTIFY KEY OBJECTIVES)

TECHNOLOGY

(CHOOSE THE RIGHT TOOLS)

RESULTS

(ACHIEVE MAXIMUM INVESTMENT VALUE)

EXECUTIVE SUMMARY

Collaboration technology solutions have maximum impact when they address your top business priorities. Whether you want to optimize team performance, enable mobile users, reach new markets or improve customer satisfaction, use the examples and framing questions in this chapter to identify your company's most pressing needs.

Then, supported by a collaborative culture and processes, you can gather the best tools to get the job done faster.

Here's something you might not expect a couple of technology executives to say: Resist the urge to rush your investment in collaboration technology. That's right. Wait until you've identified your business goals, and *then* determine the collaboration technologies—and people processes—that best support the strategy. Identify your priorities before making decisions on the best tools, not the other way around.

You can improve many cross-company business processes and activities through collaboration, enabling you to move with greater speed and flexibility to address your business priorities. Here are eight business needs that companies commonly face where collaboration technologies make a big difference.

Most companies find opportunities in more than one area, and there are many possibilities beyond this starter list:

1. Optimize team performance
2. Enable mobile users
3. Improve organizational communication and alignment

4. Expand into new markets
5. Improve customer satisfaction
6. Establish green operations
7. Increase intercompany collaboration
8. Transform your industry

How many of these needs rank high on your executive to-do list? What are your top three objectives for the year? Use the topics below to get an idea of how best to focus your approach.

1. Optimize Team Performance

Help geographically dispersed groups work across boundaries and time zones to speed business agility.

Today's virtual teams often include employees from different departments working in different regions and time zones. Video communications help members of virtual teams to build trust quickly, helping them to better execute interdependent tasks guided by shared goals that transcend functional and departmental lines. Technologies like unified communications, telepresence, social software and web conferencing help teams overcome the challenges of space and time to reach new levels of productivity. Companies that give virtual teams these tools can build trust while increasing information-sharing and accelerating the time it takes to complete a task.

Of four hundred global executives polled by the Economist Intelligence Unit, more than 75 percent work on virtual teams.[16]

These virtual teams are often ad hoc and fluid in nature, with groups coming together on the fly to complete a project and then disbanding as quickly as they formed. Before the advent of collaborative technologies, these individuals could not have found each other easily and might not even have known the others existed. But with new tools, they can tap pockets of knowledge instantly. Teams may meet every day for two weeks and then never again. Or they may meet once a month for six months, collaborating in communities and forums between those sessions. The pattern of meeting and working can be adjusted to suit the task at hand, rather than being dictated by travel schedules and costs.

How important are virtual teams to your organization? Ask yourself these questions:

- → How dispersed is our existing workforce? Do our employees work in different offices or time zones?
- → Is it easy to find expertise within the company?
- → How do we manage interactions and share information across the different departments, time zones and other boundaries within the enterprise?

2. Enable Mobile Users

Maximize the productivity and availability of mobile knowledge workers to accelerate competitive advantage.

Work has become what you do, not where you go. Executives, salespeople, consultants and other knowledge workers are leaving the cubicle to do their jobs at home or from the road. Over the next five years, most industries will move away from a location-centric work environment to a dispersed mobile world where employees are situated in the locations where they work best. Workers will bring new computing devices and expectations to the job. The integration of mobile devices and applications presents new challenges as the mobile workforce takes shape.

How do you maximize the productivity of mobile workers while controlling costs and ensuring security? It's a tall order that requires new ways of thinking about how you provide corporate IT services. Solutions for video and web conferencing, customer care, social software, unified communications, messaging and mobile applications all have a role to play.

We recently came across an energy company that applied this thinking to address issues arising at its oil well sites. When something goes wrong, a mobile petroleum expert must provide immediate analysis or advice. In the past, troubleshooting a problem meant finding the experts and physically transporting them to the well site. Now many of these expert connections occur using video-enabled collaboration tools, eliminating the downtime that drains resources while reducing operational and travel costs.

Is mobile workforce productivity a critical concern for your company? Consider these questions:

→ How, and from where, do our employees most often connect to the corporate network?
→ What communication capabilities and applications need to be enabled on mobile devices?
→ Do our employees have the necessary tools and technologies to work from multiple locations or from home?
→ How do we provide employees with flexible work hours, flexible locations and remote access to business applications?
→ How will increasing the availability and responsiveness of our mobile workers impact customer satisfaction?

3. Improve Organizational Communication and Alignment

Keep all levels of the company moving in the same direction and drive business results.

Remember when a memo was all you needed to reach the people in your organization? This one-size-fits-all approach is long gone. Leaders and managers must use all available channels to reach their increasingly dispersed workforce. Information spreads fast through online communities and social networks. This instantaneous messaging can work for or against you, depending on the situation and whether you

1 2 3 4 5 6 7 8 9 10

factor collaboration into your strategy. You need to communicate core business objectives and rapidly changing information, yet avoid the costly mistakes of overlooking channels of communication or using the wrong method at the wrong time.

As we discussed in chapter three, communicating authentically is vital. In our increasingly dispersed working environment, your message is far more authentic when it's delivered via video and reinforced through frequent virtual interactions. For example, you can:

→ Offer workers the flexibility and choice to consume information when, where and how they need it—whether in-person, virtually or on-demand
→ Build communities to improve employee engagement and understanding of shared goals
→ Manage through crisis situations by delivering information in more engaging ways at the first sign of a problem
→ Gain feedback and engage team members

When managing through a critical period, such as a turnaround or an acquisition, executives can use collaboration technology to control the message and help each part of the organization understand its role. Video plays a pivotal role in these situations. We all take difficult news much better when we hear it face-to-face. Making eye contact motivates and inspires a team in a way that text-based or audio communication cannot. And by communicating via chat sessions, virtual meetings and community posts, managers identify the needs and gauge the reactions of diverse audiences, cultures and behaviors.

How well does your organization communicate? Here are a few questions to ask:

→ Do we offer flexibility and choice for workers to consume information the way they choose?

- → Does our culture allow employees to contribute ideas and opinions or join group discussions?
- → How are we capturing employee feedback and opinions?
- → Can social media help us reach communities of interest?

4. Expand Into New Markets

Find and engage new customers around the world.

One of the most exciting business opportunities that collaboration presents is the prospect of entering new markets. Mobile, social, virtual and video technologies open up entire segments previously out of reach. Businesses that once depended on physical distribution—from university lectures to film festivals to corporate training—can reach new or broader audiences.

Consider the example of an industry conference that hosts several hundred attendees inside a convention center for a three-day show. With the right collaboration tools, that same conference can become a global community of several thousand virtual members who sustain the conversation throughout the year. Imagine the incremental revenue of engaging in pre-conference community building, live video streaming and post-conference video sharing. No longer limited by distribution, you can transform the event into a dynamic, evolving two-way dialogue and bring your brand to life.

Are you ready to grow your business into new areas? Here are a few questions to ask:

- → Which new customer segments or new markets do we want to reach?
- → How do we currently serve remote customers?
- → How might we re-imagine our current offering and deliver it in a virtual format?

5. Improve Customer Satisfaction

Improve the quality and efficiency of customer communications and engagement to create more loyal customers.

Every customer interaction is a chance to enhance or hurt your brand. A frustrating interaction with the contact center, negative online reviews, poor handling of a safety recall or a limited presence in social channels will have a ripple effect across the company. Having the flexibility to make adjustments based on feedback from customers provides an opportunity to separate yourself from competitors.

EXPERT ADVICE ON CUSTOMER EXPERIENCE

"Happy customers share their positive experience with four or five people. Dissatisfied customers will complain about their negative experience to between nine and twelve people."

–from *Extreme Management* by Mark Stevens, Grand Central Publishing, 2002

The expectations of connected customers have flipped the world around. Your job is to deliver information, products and services anywhere, anytime and on the customer's terms. With loyalty a fickle commodity, businesses must keep the conversation fresh while analyzing what's being said in the most influential communities. The way you handle customer interactions is more critical than ever to the future of your organization.

When companies put unified communications, web conferencing, customer-interaction applications and social software in place, they allow customer-service representatives to get the right information at the right time, and thus reduce problem resolution times. Faster problem solving improves customer-service agents' productivity, so they can help more customers in the same amount of time. Personalized interactions forge stronger relationships. And social media monitoring helps companies listen to what customers are saying and respond quickly to their feedback.

Are you ready to explore how more collaborative customer care applies to your business? Start with these questions:

- → Do we need a way to scale specialized subject-matter experts to reach customers without inflating headcount?
- → What is our strategy for increasing first-call resolution and improving customer satisfaction?
- → How can rich and frequent video communications increase intimacy and aid in building trust with our customers?
- → Are we actively monitoring what the market is saying about us or our competition, and do we have a way to quickly address customer complaints made on social media outlets?

6. Enhance Green Operations

Reduce costs with planet-friendly solutions.

Large enterprises face extreme pressure to operate in more sustainable ways. With energy costs on the rise, regulatory requirements increasing and concern for the planet ranking high among consumers' priorities, a green strategy is essential. Companies are judged every day on their commitment to protect the environment, and advanced collaboration solutions offer a path to achieve the goal. Plus, it's the right thing to do.

Telepresence and other video and web conferencing solutions reduce the need for business travel, enable teleworking and create opportunities for better use of office space. Executive reviews, product-design workshops and employee-training sessions all can shift to the virtual model. Unified communications connect employees anywhere, anytime and decrease the need for physical office space. The ability to share working drafts of a presentation or engineering schematic in a virtual meeting lessens the need for reviewers to print and send paper copies. Together, these steps shape an approach that is more environmentally aware.

The Value of Teleworking

A study of people working from home at least one day a week found that telecommuting saved 840 million gallons of gasoline per year and reduced greenhouse gas emissions by 14 million tons annually. The report calculated the total savings in electricity to be nine to 14 billion kilowatt-hours a year—approximately equivalent to the energy used by one million U.S. households.[17]

For our part, Cisco has pledged to reduce its carbon emissions 25 percent by 2012 and already has documented 462,637 metric tons of emissions saved since we began measuring the impact of our collaboration solutions in 2006. Recognizing that business travel and commuting have high financial and environmental costs, we use unified communications, telepresence and web conferencing to make virtual meetings a viable alternative to meeting face-to-face.

The efforts have produced significant results: Telepresence alone had generated $857 million in travel cost savings (based on an average of four participants per meeting and $1,000 average cost per trip). We've avoided travel for more than 200,000 meetings since Cisco introduced the technology. As an added benefit, collaboration has compressed our sales cycle too. Based on a sample analysis of 326 sales opportunities, we believe telepresence reduced the average Cisco sales cycle time by just under ten percent.

To apply collaboration technology to a green initiative, consider these questions:

- → What are our carbon reduction goals?
- → What is the occupancy utilization in our real estate today? What percentage of our workforce telecommutes?
- → What is the value to our company of being perceived as a sustainability leader?

1 2 3 4 5 6 7 8 9 10

7. Increase Intercompany Collaboration

Improve collaboration outside the firewall and across the entire supply chain.

In a highly connected global marketplace, businesses need to collaborate externally with partners, suppliers, vendors, investors and customers. Intercompany collaboration is essential for sales and marketing, technical support, joint research and development, auditing and legal matters. A manufacturer, for example, may source materials from a partner in one country, assemble products in another country and sell to buyers in yet another. A software developer may team up with researchers, resellers and systems integrators to ensure its product will work for its target customers. Each part of the supply chain requires communication between companies. The key is to enable them with the same collaboration tools that you have inside your own company and embrace the same people processes outlined in previous chapters to enhance the effectiveness of virtual teams.

Intercompany teams meet often, over long periods of time, to work on critical business issues. They need better tools than email and audio conferences to enable true

Fifty-one percent of respondents said they are part of a permanent intercompany team, and 67 percent said they work on externally facing teams that meet at least a few times a month, according to a survey by Forrester Research.[18]

collaboration. The challenge is in how to facilitate the kind of communication you've established within your intracompany teams across firewalls and among different IT systems and environments.

When encountering intercompany communication challenges, employees depend on management to step in and find a solution. If you don't provide the right tools, your employees and those of your partners may well take matters into their own hands and find a better way to work. And this can pose potentially serious security challenges.

How do you know if your employees need better intercompany collaboration tools? Start with these questions:

→ How often do our employees interact with other organizations in our supply chain?
→ What tools do we use to facilitate intercompany meetings?
→ How secure are these collaboration tools?
→ What benefits would we realize if we enabled more complex interactions outside the firewall?

8. Transform Your Industry

Change the rules of the game with innovation fueled by collaboration.

When applied aggressively, collaboration technology can transform an industry. Collaboration pioneers already have made radical improvements across all kinds of industries by reinventing how business gets done. Highly personalized banking, distance learning, distributed global research and development and better interactions between governments and their constituents are just a few examples of what's possible today.

Here's where we see collaboration revolutionizing business. It's always exciting to see true visionaries apply collaboration technologies within their companies in ways that advance the entire industry—and keep competitors playing catch-up. Like the Internet before it, collaboration has the potential to transform every industry. It's just a question of who gets there first.

Where are the opportunities to innovate in your industry and gain a first-mover advantage? Consider these questions:

→ What factors constrain the pace of innovation in our company or our industry? And what kind of advantage would we gain by innovating faster?
→ What new business models can we enable with virtual teams, mobile productivity and stronger customer interactions?
→ What is holding our industry back, and how could improved collaboration overcome these barriers?
→ How are competitors reinventing our industry today? Where are the opportunities to leap ahead?

CASE STUDY

JW Marriott Marquis Miami Reinvents the Travel Experience

A hotel for the 21st century, the new JW Marriott Marquis Miami redefines what it means to work on the road. While most hotels install technology to meet the basic needs of travelers, this hotel's leadership team asked a critical question: How can we support the lifestyle of our customers today and in the future?

They wanted to create a hotel that was unique in the market and would command attention from customers and the industry. They selected pervasive video technology to alter the company's approach to business, entertainment and safety. In the lobby, guests use lifelike telepresence to talk to a virtual concierge for information about the hotel. Business travelers host virtual meetings using an advanced telepresence system that

1 2 3 4 5 6 7 8 9 10

accommodates up to six people per location. In guest rooms, wireless IP touch-screen phones provide the interface for ordering breakfast, checking the weather and setting wake-up calls. Guests can even use their iPhones to change television channels just like they can at home.

Guests have 100 percent network connectivity throughout the property. No more connecting in the lobby only to lose the connection when you head back to your room. People walk and work at the same time, and they can have multiple devices going all at once. There is nothing to slow them down.

Most impressive of all, the collaboration platform approach means that hotel management now has the flexibility to create new services and meet customer needs as they arise. They can turn facility features on and off and provide guest services instantly. JW Marriott Marquis Miami management understands that guests continually redefine the standard for exceptional service, and the hospitality leader's ability to keep pace with demands will mean the difference between winning new business and losing it to another hotel.

Aim High—You Won't Regret It

Don't limit your vision to the experiences we've described. There are infinite possibilities and combinations to help your organization adapt more quickly to meet its business objectives. Naturally, the collaboration journey will be different for every organization.

The important thing is to think creatively. Wherever you choose to focus that initial effort, you are bound to realize tangible benefits. And remember, the more pervasive collaboration becomes, the more powerful its effect will be—both inside and outside the firewall.

60 SECOND WRAP

:00 There are at least eight common opportunities where companies find great value in collaboration:

01 Optimize team performance by helping dispersed teams work effectively across boundaries and time zones

02 Empower mobile users to be more productive, available and responsive to customers to accelerate competitive advantage

03 Communicate effectively throughout the company to align the organization and drive business results

04 Expand into new markets by reaching remote customers with new virtual offers

05 Enhance the customer experience to create more satisfied and loyal customers

06 Establish green operations through reduced travel and more sustainable work practices

07 Increase intercompany collaboration by extending new technology beyond the firewall and across the entire supply chain

08 Transform your industry through new business models enabled by technology-driven innovation

:50 You can find opportunities in more than one area, and there are many other possibilities. Don't be afraid to chart your own path to the collaborative organization.

9

WHAT IS THE TRUE PAYBACK OF COLLABORATION?

Get the maximum return on your investments—from operational and productivity improvements to competitive advantage.

STRATEGIC DIFFERENTIATION

RETURN ON INVESTMENT

PRODUCTIVITY GAINS

OPERATIONAL SAVINGS

EXECUTIVE SUMMARY

As you plot the next steps in your organization's collaboration journey, it helps to understand the returns that are possible. You can measure the return on collaboration investments in three ways: operational savings, productivity gains and strategic differentiation.

Follow a few guiding principles to ensure that you realize the full potential of your collaboration strategy.

With so many technologies to choose from and so many types of collaborative activities, how do you decide where to begin, or what to try next? And how do you know if collaboration is worth the investment?

As INSEAD and University of California at Berkeley Professor Morten T. Hansen wrote, "The goal of collaboration is not collaboration itself, but great results."[19] Every leader wants to measure the tangible benefits of an investment. Working with many of our customers, we've developed a framework for assessing the true value of collaboration. Return on investment (ROI) for collaboration falls into three distinct categories:

→ **Operational ROI** allows you to assess how collaboration eliminates or avoids costs associated with running your business. You might cut travel, reduce infrastructure needs, lower bandwidth or energy costs, save on office space and so on. Collaboration can replace or reduce the need for many of these types of costs.

→ **Productivity ROI** refers to savings generated from more efficient processes, accelerated decision making and reduced cycle times. Collaboration can lead to significant productivity gains in any number of ways, such as optimizing within lines of business or matching expertise to opportunities early on.

- → **Strategic ROI** can be the hardest to measure, but perhaps the most transformative. This kind of ROI occurs when collaboration enables your business to take a giant leap forward in areas like enhancing customer satisfaction and loyalty, speeding up innovation, introducing new business models or entering new markets. These types of changes can also reshape an industry in fundamental ways.

You Get Out What You Put In

According to a global study of business and IT leaders conducted by Frost & Sullivan, the return on a collaboration investment becomes progressively greater as more advanced tools are deployed and a better collaborative culture takes shape. Consider the results:

- → *Basic collaborators* enjoy almost a threefold return on deployment, suggesting that even minimal collaboration capabilities can be used to generate some modest return.
- → *Intermediate collaborators* see a 25 percent greater impact than basic collaborators, with a return of 3.6 times their investment.
- → *Advanced collaborators* see more than two times the impact as basic collaborators, at just over six times the return on their deployment.[21]

The average return on collaboration is nearly four times a company's initial investment.[20]

Even a low level of adoption results in moderate performance gains. Progressively better collaboration yields progressively better performance and returns. But everyone can benefit from the collaboration tools they put in place. No matter what level of technology adoption, you'll experience greater benefits if that adoption is supported by cultural and process transformation in an integrated approach.

Next, let's look more closely at each category along the ROI continuum.

YOU GET OUT WHAT YOU PUT IN[22]

Even basic collaborators realized an almost three-fold return on the deployment of collaboration technologies, according to a global study of business and IT leaders conducted by Frost & Sullivan, while advanced collaborators experienced a more than six-fold return.

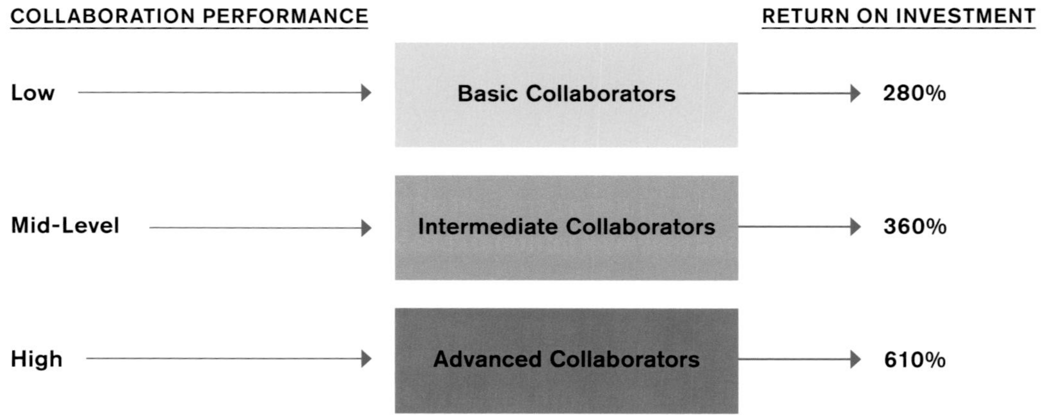

Operational ROI: Cost Avoidance and Cost Reduction

When a company uses telepresence to have face-to-face meetings while avoiding travel costs, or it migrates from a dated PBX system to IP communications to reduce IT infrastructure costs, the principles of operational ROI are at work. In another example, web conferencing enables employees to work from a home office, reducing a company's office space requirements. Operational ROI is hard-dollar savings that go right to the bottom line. That means it's the easiest type of return to measure.

Research shows the vast majority of companies investing in collaboration experience a positive return on their investment. Among six vertical industries that were measured in a 2010 study by Salire Partners—financial services, government, health care, high tech, manufacturing and retail—all saw positive return on collaboration over a five-year period, from 120 percent to more than 200 percent.

1 2 3 4 5 6 7 8 9 10

RETURN ON COLLABORATION BY INDUSTRY[23]

VERTICAL INDUSTRY	AVERAGE PAYBACK IN MONTHS	FIVE-YEAR ROI
Financial	30	174%
Government	33	154%
Health Care & Pharma	31	139%
High Tech	21	204%
Manufacturing	33	159%
Retail	40	120%

The same study found that small and large companies alike enjoyed favorable operational ROI regardless of their location in the world, with the average payback taking place within just a couple of years.

ROI BY NUMBER OF EMPLOYEES[24]

SIZE OF ORGANIZATION	AVERAGE PAYBACK IN MONTHS	FIVE-YEAR ROI
Less than 1,000	37	99%
1,000–5,000	27	173%
5,000–10,000	37	171%
10,000–25,000	30	173%
More than 25,000	35	127%

Productivity ROI: Business Unit Optimization and Accelerated Business Decisions

Productivity ROI is the heart and soul of operational excellence. As analysts at McKinsey & Company say, "Raising the productivity of employees whose jobs can't be automated is the next great performance challenge—and the stakes are high."[25]

To stay on top, your organization has to be more productive every year. You must improve day-to-day operations within business lines and increase response time and decision making. The only way to do this is by removing barriers that prevent your business from moving forward.

Determine what you're measuring, establish benchmarks against which you'll measure, set challenging goals and create accountability to achieve those goals.

There are many ways to drive productivity ROI. Consider these questions:

→ Can you accelerate the hiring process by using video tools to eliminate travel for interviewing job candidates? Could you land a high-value prospect before a competitor discovers the talent?

- → Would communities of interest within your organization enable employees to locate individuals with the expertise to close a sale?
- → Could your product development teams use Web conferencing and virtual collaborative workspaces to reduce review cycles and get to market faster?
- → Can you collapse the time it takes to make important decisions?

By strengthening the human interactions inherent in your business, collaboration tools play a large part in establishing, increasing or maintaining your competitive advantage in the marketplace.

CASE STUDY

Productivity Improvements Accommodate Phenomenal Growth at MODEC

Sometimes an impossible challenge brings out the best in people. MODEC—a general contractor specializing in engineering, construction and operations of deep-water platforms for oil and gas—experienced this effect when it won a staggering amount of new business that required its workforce to triple in a matter of months. CIO Ed Flavin had to keep the underlying infrastructure from crumbling under the weight of this exponential growth. "We were either going to be very successful or we were going to fail miserably," he recalls.

Unable to hire and train new people quickly enough, MODEC realized the only answer was to help experienced employees work smarter. Thus began a quest to figure out how collaboration could enable higher productivity among engineers located in Tokyo and Singapore and managers in the United States.

In the past, completing an engineering drawing took up to eight weeks, with some 50 engineers in different time zones making changes by hand,

1 2 3 4 5 6 7 8 9 10

scanning new versions and sharing them via a file transfer protocol site. Flavin saw the potential to accelerate this process with collaboration tools, but he had to balance the needs of two distinct groups in the workforce.

A group of thirty-something engineers just out of grad school wanted to use real-time online collaboration spaces, instant messaging, Web cams, 3-D and four monitors each. But the majority of MODEC employees were older professionals with decades of experience and less tolerance for new technology. They were more comfortable picking up a phone, printing a 2-D CAD drawing and red-lining it with a pencil.

How could MODEC get these groups to collaborate? Flavin believed the answer was to provide a menu of options available to all, without forcing the technology on anyone. "Not everybody works the same way," says Flavin, "So we said, 'We're going to give you as many possible tools as we can afford and that we think are going to add value, and you choose the ones that are going to make you the most successful in your job.'"

If you used to measure cycle times of critical aspects of the business in weeks and now you measure them in days, the power of collaboration becomes remarkably clear.

Unified communications, Web conferencing and a wired and wireless network were just the beginning. Before long, engineers were collaborating online, joining after-hours work calls from home, sharing their desktops and making changes in real time. Now, when a decision needs to be made, everyone agrees right then and there in the meeting. And that multi-week process for engineering drawings? MODEC cut it down to several days.

This kind of collaboration allows MODEC engineers to work together without putting people on a plane for 22 hours from Houston to Singapore. Collaboration technology has bridged a cultural divide, and higher productivity has enabled the company to manage remarkably well through a dramatic growth period.

COLLABORATION IMPACT ACROSS YOUR ORGANIZATION[26]

All functions within your organization benefit from investing in collaboration technologies, according to a global survey of business and IT leaders conducted by Frost & Sullivan. The more advanced your collaboration efforts are, the greater the benefit.

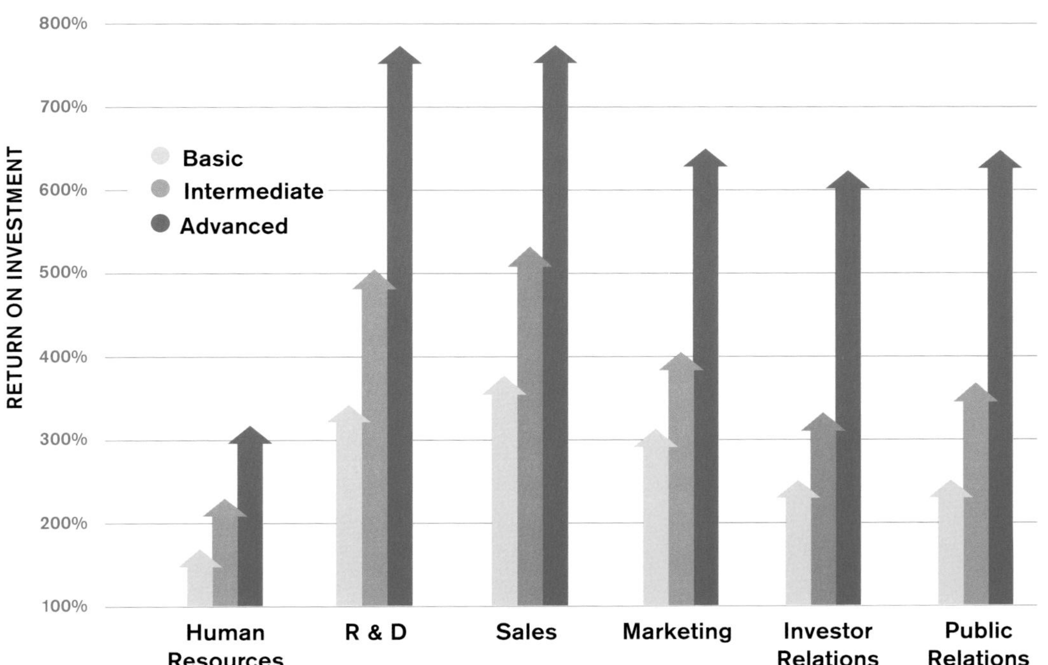

More Interactions, Greater Benefit

When we look across various functional areas of a business, we find an interesting trend related to productivity ROI: The greatest impact of collaboration occurs in areas where the largest numbers of people interact to produce value. Sales teams and research and development groups, where many-to-many relatioonships are essential to making good decisions, are prime examples. But all business units can

The network effect for collaboration: More interactions mean greater benefit to the company.

benefit from increased collaboration, according to research from Frost & Sullivan, and the more interactions increase, the greater the benefit to the company.[27] This is the network effect for collaboration, and once you understand how it works, you can use it to your advantage.

Strategic ROI: Customer Satisfaction and Business Transformation

Beyond these quantifiable operational and productivity gains, collaboration can set a company apart in its market. What is the value of pioneering a new business model, entering a new market or forging new customer relationships that foster true loyalty? This is strategic ROI. It's about transformational changes that create long-term value for customers and competitive advantage for your business. It can even mean the reinvention of an entire industry.

One way to measure strategic ROI is through the lens of customer satisfaction and loyalty. Research shows that collaboration improves customer relationships. A study by the Aberdeen Group found that 53 percent of "best-in-class companies" from a collaboration perspective reported an improvement in customer satisfaction."[28] Why are customers more satisfied? They can reach a company representative more quickly and, if needed, gain access to knowledgeable subject-matter experts who resolve their problems or requests faster. This is powerful stuff in the eyes of your customers..

Duke University Transforms Higher Education

Duke University is one of most progressive universities when it comes to collaboration. With a combination of social media, telepresence and other technologies, the university is virtualizing knowledge transfer and changing the face of higher education.

Professor Tony O'Driscoll teaches in a cross-continent MBA program for 160 students enrolled in Duke University's Fuqua School of Business. The context of the school's dilemma, he explains, is a globalization challenge with a distributed group of constituents. Students are based in 30 different countries, and they come together as a group for 10-day residencies six times a year in places like Shanghai, London, Dubai, Delhi and St. Petersburg.

Constrained by the limited amount of face time with students in the program, Professor O'Driscoll wondered what technologies Duke could bring to bear to help the team get work done at a distance. The answer: Change the way students prepare for residencies using interactive reading packets.

In the past, students received a large box of pre-reading material, dubbed "the box of doom," which they had to read before beginning each residency. The professor had no way of knowing whether books were being read and understood. Often, precious time during residencies meant for group discussion and issues-based learning was spent getting lagging students up to speed on the basics.

A social media approach has transformed the process for professor and students alike. Professor O'Driscoll now posts all educational materials—not just books but articles, videos and other media—within an online community called *The Commons.* There, he can see who is reading what and view comments from students. He can take polls, pose questions and host virtual meetings. Students can discuss issues among themselves as well.

By the time students arrive for a residency, they are informed and ready for higher learning that is more thought-provoking and conceptual, without being bogged down with material better learned before the group convenes.

This is a fundamentally different way of learning—more hands-on, more visual, more collaborative. Social media facilitates issues-based discussion instead of memorizing facts. Just imagine what these graduates will accomplish when they re-enter the workplace.

Innovation at Duke University doesn't stop there. A first-of-its-kind

YOU GET (

WHAT YOU

OUT

PUT IN.

virtual lecture hall means Duke can tap outside expertise and bring guest lecturers face-to-face with students via telepresence. Business school students get access to professors, business leaders and respected minds located around the globe. The CEO of Honda can join a class on international business. Jack Welch might address a course on leadership. This opens up new doors for education. In the process, it puts Duke in a leadership position.

Industry by Industry: Collaboration Makes a Difference

In just about every industry, collaboration enables a variety of improvements ranging from basic efficiency gains to industry-wide transformation. Here are a few examples:

No matter what industry you're in, collaboration tools can be an agent of change.

- → **Financial services.** We all know that the days of waiting in line at the bank are long gone. Today, you can use a virtual mortgage lender, make a deposit on your smart phone, and speak to video service representatives who have access to your banking history and can suggest new products based on your personal needs and history. Collaboration streamlines operations, offers customers a multichannel experience and provides on-demand expertise.
- → **Health care.** In health care, telemedicine brings experts together with patients to enhance the consultation and treatment processes. Nurses and doctors are mobile and have fast access to information they need. Collaboration can help decrease patient wait times, increase clinical safety and provide better visibility into staffing requirements. All of these improvements can lower the cost of providing care while ensuring better patient care.
- → **Manufacturing.** Here, the primary benefit is innovation. Companies develop products in one country, manufacture them in another and market them in yet another without skipping a beat. Everyone has complete

visibility into the process, and the work never stops. It's a transparent, seamless supply chain.

- **Retail.** In retail, collaboration changes the way goods are made and sold. Virtual fitting rooms take time and space out of the equation, as designers review designs and choose fabrics without traveling to Europe and Asia. A process that once took a month can be done in a matter of hours. Meanwhile, at the other end of the retail cycle, new contact center capabilities offer real-time sensing of Twitter feeds from within a store, so retailers can send highly targeted offers to the mobile devices of consumers inside the store. For consumers, the result is a personalized shopping experience from start to finish.
- **Government.** Federal and local governments use collaboration to enhance public safety, drive efficiency in times of budget constraint and improve the citizen experience with 24-hour access to many services. Police are using mobility and presence solutions to improve public safety. Courts are using virtual trials that include video conferencing technology to save on transportation costs and accelerate the trial process. And prisons are taking advantage of telepresence to bring human services to inmates on premises.

Collaboration Is Not a Project

The pace of innovation in collaboration is faster than anyone can comprehend or predict. How do you protect your investments for the future? Follow these guiding principles:

- **Take a holistic approach.** Deploying an architectural approach to collaboration allows you to integrate IP Communications, conferencing, mobile software, messaging, enterprise social software and customer care into a flexible and open portfolio that evolves with your business. Be sure to plan for future growth and changes in devices, applications or strategy.

→ **Bring video, mobility and social software into everything you do.** These three technologies represent the future of collaboration. Address each of them proactively as you plan your collaboration strategy. They are critical to your long-term success.
→ **Think big.** Plan an intercompany strategy that addresses the entire supply chain. Get your partners, suppliers and customers involved to maximize collaboration results.
→ **Understand deployment options.** There are many ways to extend the benefits of collaboration to your organization. You can host solutions on site, through public or private clouds or in a blended model. Look into a virtual desktop experience for unprecedented flexibility and security.
→ **Stay true to your business goals.** Collaboration works best when you use it to support your organization's shared goals and business priorities. Develop relationships with your stakeholders to understand their needs and how collaboration can further those goals.
→ **Don't wait.** You can't afford to stop innovating, even when it feels overwhelming or risky. But you don't need to plot the entire journey. You will learn along the way and implement course corrections as you go.

60 SECOND WRAP

:00 There are three distinct categories of collaboration ROI—operational ROI, productivity ROI and strategic ROI—and companies are achieving results in each of these categories today.

:10 Operational ROI allows you to eliminate or avoid costs associated with running your business.

:15 Productivity ROI comes into play when we talk about savings generated from more efficient processes, accelerated decision making and reduced cycle times.

:25 Strategic ROI occurs when collaboration enables your business to take a giant leap forward in areas like customer satisfaction and loyalty, faster innovation, new business models or new markets.

:30 Even a low level of collaboration adoption results in moderate performance gains. Progressively better collaboration yields progressively better performance and returns.

:35 To maximize the potential of your collaboration strategy, take a holistic approach, focus on shared business goals and get started now.

:40 The greatest impact of collaboration occurs in areas where the largest numbers of people interact to produce value.

:50 Remember that collaboration is a journey, not a project. Allow for future growth and changes in devices, applications or strategy.

10

THE TIME IS NOW

Take the next step on your journey as a collaborative leader.

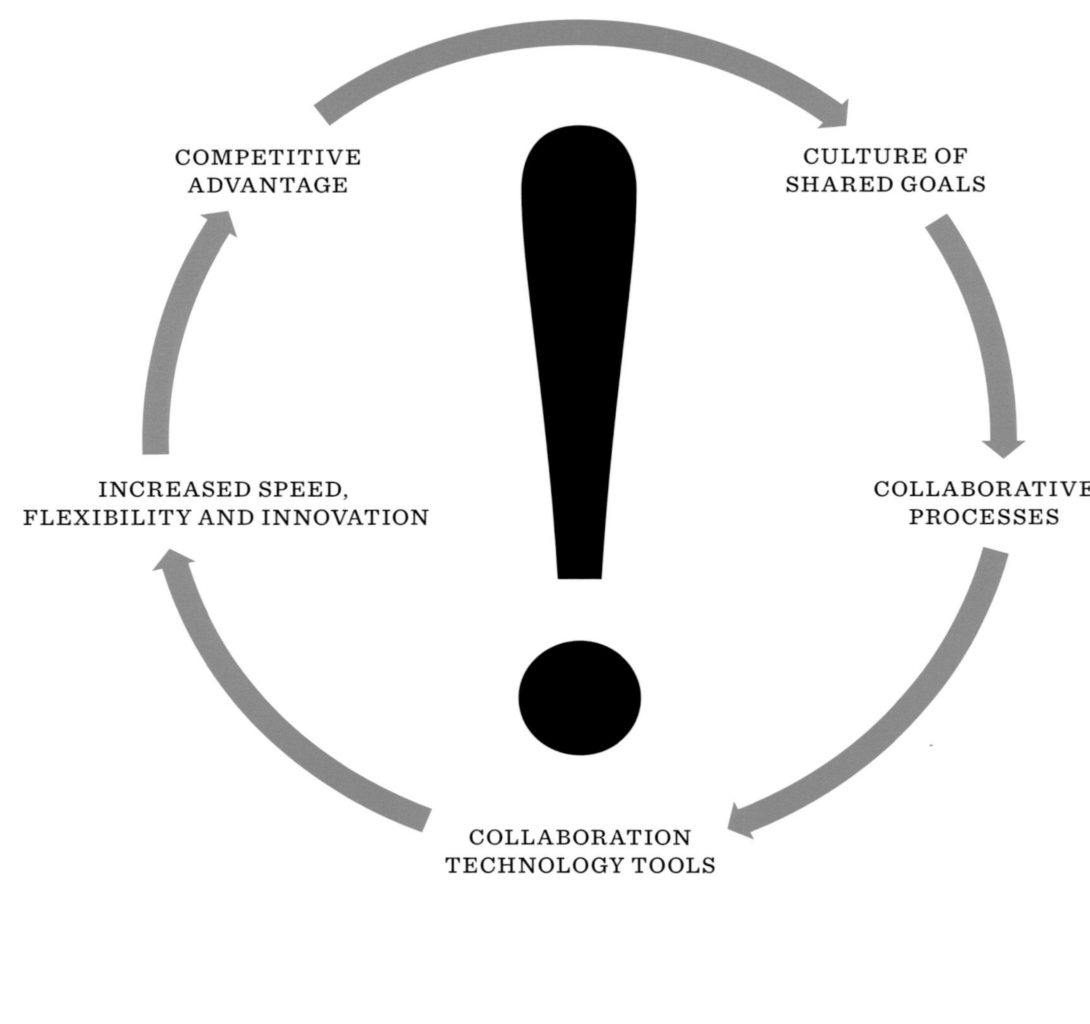
COMPETITIVE ADVANTAGE
CULTURE OF SHARED GOALS
COLLABORATIVE PROCESSES
COLLABORATION TECHNOLOGY TOOLS
INCREASED SPEED, FLEXIBILITY AND INNOVATION

EXECUTIVE SUMMARY

A collaboration strategy is essential to achieving business agility in the coming decade. Assess your collaboration readiness by looking at your corporate culture, people processes and technology infrastructure.

Then encourage collaboration across your organization.

Twenty years ago, Cisco built routers in a 10,000-square-foot manufacturing facility on First Street in San Jose, California. Today, we collaborate with external manufacturing partners around the globe. We partner with other companies to deliver new innovations to our customers. For this business model to work, we have had to overcome geographic, cultural and departmental differences. We work in virtual communities that span time zones, cultures, languages and generations. Video technology brings us together when we can't be face-to-face.

As we learn how to operate in a hyper-connected economy, we are experimenting with new, spontaneous work formations. We often work in swarms of 20 to 30 people and empower employees to make fast decisions. We know when to apply decentralized thinking, and when to revert to a command-and-control approach. Collaboration has enabled a significant transformation, and we are not alone.

A Paris suburb credits its economic turnaround to a new collaboration infrastructure, while a global nutritional products company increases sales through a social media-based data mining program. In Mexico, an insurance provider uses telepresence to enhance training and drive incremental sales. Engineering companies accelerate their product-design processes by collaborating with video conferencing, while energy companies identify untapped field capacity through a tighter link between global experts and local resources. Auto companies can manufacture anywhere, gaining access to emerging markets, while hospitals revolutionize patient care and universities build learning environments of the future.

EXPERT TIP ON GOALS

"A unifying goal has power only if all relevant groups need to pull together to make it a reality."

—from *Collaboration* by Morten T. Hansen, Harvard Business Press, 2009

What can a collaboration strategy do for you? The time to explore the answer is now. Assign a leadership team to steer your collaboration-building effort. Invite employees from all levels of the organization as well as various functional groups to participate. Be sure to represent your various geographic regions and a range of workers from the youngest to the oldest, so that all points of view are included. Communicate the shared goal of becoming an adaptive enterprise. Get everyone focused on achieving organizational productivity and fostering an environment that adjusts to the individual's situation. Together, the team will find ways to build collective knowledge and increase utilization with unrivaled creativity. Set your sights on the goal, then begin to shape your culture, processes and technology architecture to get there.

Can you identify shared goals and foster a culture that encourages your entire organization to rally together to achieve them? Are those goals communicated clearly to everyone involved?

Reexamine business processes such as training, development and recruiting in the context of collaboration. Provide the right experience for the task at hand. Eliminate overlaps and redundancies to minimize internal competition for resources and allow your organization to reallocate those resources in a more beneficial way.

Spend some time with your company's IT leaders to conduct an inventory of your existing collaboration environments. Find out what technologies are already in place, and who is using them. What tools are available to employees, partners and others in the enterprise ecosystem? Understand how these physical environments differ depending on location. Do telecommuting employees have the same capabilities as employees working from headquarters? Do partners have the necessary IT environments to participate in new collaboration initiatives? Is the necessary security in place to protect valuable corporate assets? Do these solutions give your organization some headroom for what collaboration will look like in the future?

Above all, remember that the more leaders model collaborative behavior, the more employees will adopt those behaviors and the more collaboration will proliferate throughout your organization. Here are some steps you can take to encourage collaboration across the company:

EXPERT TIP ON BARRIERS

1 2 3 4 5 6 7 8 9 10

"Believe it or not, the biggest barriers to collaboration are not the technical ones...but the human ones. Two people who don't want to talk to each other are still not going to want to talk to each other even if you give them all kinds of collaboration tools. The soft stuff is the hard stuff."

—Dr. Thomas W. Malone, author of *The Future of Work*[29]

→ **Focus on collaboration readiness.** Divide collaboration readiness into two areas: the environment (the necessary tools and processes) and ability (the training, cultural awareness and willingness to collaborate). Your collaborative evolution will go through natural phases, from your first investigative attempts through more thorough adoption of collaborative practices and—eventually—high-performance collaboration. Think about what tools you're going to use, and how your processes need to change to support collaboration. Some processes may not change much but others, especially those that revolve around how people interact with each other, are ripe for transformation. Also, consider how things like training must change in order to foster increased collaboration. People often benefit from participation-based training when it comes to collaboration readiness. Lastly, ask yourself how policies must change in order to reflect more collaborative business practices.

→ **Develop collaborative decision-making processes.** Establish a common vocabulary for making decisions. Start communicating this common vocabulary and decision-making framework at the executive level. Then migrate it throughout the rest of the company once you're satisfied that it's working well. Use executive development programs to implement the new model.

→ **Encourage early adopters.** Some people will immediately use collaboration tools and techniques as they become available. Encourage their experimentation, and ask them to show you what works and what doesn't. Your efforts will be much more powerful if you recruit early adopters from all levels of the organization. While you're at it, become an early adopter yourself.

EXPERT TIP ON EARLY ADOPTERS

"Believers are early and spontaneous adopters, who for some reason quickly see the benefits of the new product and switch to it. Managers can leverage believers by turning them into internal champions and evangelists."

—from *Enterprise 2.0* by Dr. Andrew McAfee, Harvard Business Press, 2009

→ **Expand incentives to reward collaboration.** While you're not likely to abandon individual performance measures when determining compensation, if you're serious about collaboration, it makes sense to reward people who collaborate well. This could mean adding a collaboration metric to individual performance measures or creating high-profile recognition or award programs to celebrate collaboration. Tap into what motivates people within your culture, including not only compensation and other rewards but also recognition and reputation-building opportunities, and begin to motivate people to work together more.

→ **Remove functional, political and process barriers.** Identify and address any barriers that prevent employees, partners and customers from taking advantage of collaborative systems. As Morten T. Hansen points out in his Q&A in an earlier chapter, common barriers include the *not invented here* syndrome, information hoarding, problems finding information that's needed and transferring complicated knowledge from one team to another. These barriers often exist at the executive level, and it will take some effort to remove them. But asking an organization to behave more collaboratively without removing obstacles that are in the way will result in widespread frustration and paralysis.

→ **Communicate changes and stay involved.** Nothing drives collaborative business practices like letting your people know that senior leadership is serious about it—and committed for the long haul. By consistently communicating process and policy changes and providing data-driven and anecdotal updates about progress along the way, you can help to make collaboration a defining attribute of your organizational culture.

→ **Continually improve the model.** Collaboration is a journey, not a project. Fine-tune what you have and look for ways to create a single, harmonious organization—one that is aligned to a shared vision and working toward realizing that vision every day. Chart your progress by measuring the time it takes to complete certain types of tasks, diagramming the relationships of your social networks and getting feedback from the field. Survey the people who are participating in collaborative business practices to get a sense of what is working and what is not. Compare work and information flows and look for bottlenecks. Focus on adapting ways to remove these bottlenecks to keep things moving.

The challenge to do more with less is not new, but pervasive mobile, social, virtual and video technologies have raised the stakes and altered the playing field for good. As Dr. Thomas W. Malone tells us, "The world is not a sleepy place. Companies are vying with each other for every possible advantage, for every slice of customer attention and every dollar of revenue."[30]

In this highly unpredictable environment, it's not enough to do one thing better than your competitors. You need to change your organization so that it can adapt rapidly to whatever opportunities or threats the market delivers. What new business models, strategies or processes will your company invent tomorrow?

Collaboration is the new imperative. It's the only way to accelerate innovation, improve agility, increase adaptability and cut costs all at once. We believe collaboration is the most important investment of the decade. Your competitors know this. And they want to get ahead. It's time to put this book down, roll up your sleeves and get started.

NOW GO DO IT!

ACKNOWLEDGEMENTS

Not surprisingly, it takes a tremendous amount of collaboration to produce a book. First and foremost, we'd like to thank our editors, Molly Davis and Ewan Morrison, who helped us with this book from start to finish. They, along with the core team of Connie Dudum, Noelle Resare, Greg Thomas and Cedric Warde, were instrumental in bringing this book to life.

We'd like to thank an esteemed group of leading thinkers who generously shared with us their perspectives on collaboration: Peter Guber, Morten Hansen, Brad Holst, Thomas Malone, Andrew McAfee, Tony O'Driscoll, Marshall Van Alstyne and Greg Simpson.

We'd also like to thank the progressive organizations that openly shared their own collaboration experiences with us: Best Buy, Duke University, General Electric, JW Marriott Marquis Miami, Kohn Pedersen Fox, MODEC, Nottingham University Hospitals and Republic Services.

There are a number of individuals within Cisco who contributed important ideas and support, including some of our most respected leaders: Terry Anderson, Chris Beveridge, Brian Boeggeman, James Brooks, Ross Camp, John Chambers, Lisa Clark, Dora Ferrell, Florence Germono, Jeanette Gibson, Brian Gin, Carol Guerard, Maureen Griffin,

Nicole Hall, Sarah Halper, Mary Hunter, Jodi Krause, Kelly Lang, Bernard Lee, Lynn Lucas, Koushi Merchant, Amy Nettleton Grassi, Julie O'Brien, Minh Pham, Laura Powers, Ellie Ruano, Jeanna Soden, Jon Stine, Ali Stokes, Karen Tillman, Jamie Walton, Padmasree Warrior and Julianne Whitelaw.

We'd also like to thank our superb content development and creative partners: Eric Adams, Nikki Goth Itoi, Lightbulb Press, Volume and Paul Wearing.

Last but not least, we thank our families for their continued support and understanding. We have both dedicated a good many waking hours to the subject of collaboration—sometimes at the expense of precious family time: Debbie Wiese, Brett Wiese, Abby Wiese, Katelyn Wiese, Loretta Stagnitto, Annie Ricci and Jake Ricci.

NOTES

1 http://en.wikipedia.org/wiki/Six_Sigma

2 Established by multiple online sources

3 T. A. Judge, C.J. Thoresen, J.E. Bono, G.K. Patton, "The job satisfaction-job performance relationship: A qualitative and quantitative review," *Psychological Bulletin*, 2001

4 Jennifer Reingold, "Can P&G Make Money in Places Where People Earn $2 a Day?" *Fortune Magazine* blog, January 6, 2011, http://features.blogs.fortune.cnn.com/2011/01/06/can-pg-make-money-in-places-where-people-earn-2-a-day/

5 Michael V. Copeland, "Reid Hastings: Leader of the Pack," *Fortune Magazine*, November 18, 2010

6 http://en.wikipedia.org/wiki/Balanced_Scorecard

7 "The Challenges of Working in Virtual Teams," a report published by RW3, 2010, http://rw-3.com/VTSReportv7.pdf

8 Morten T. Hansen, *Collaboration: How leaders avoid the traps, create unity, and reap big results,* Harvard Business Press, 2009

9 Thomas W. Malone, original interview

10 "Gartner highlights key predictions for IT organizations and users in 2010 and beyond," a press release published by Gartner, January 13, 2010

11 Cisco Visual Networking Index

12 Google earnings conference call, Second Quarter 2011

13 Cisco Visual Networking Index

14 "Delivering the New Collaboration Experience," a study conducted by Cisco, November 2010

15 "The New Collaborative Workspace," a white paper published by Cisco, June 2011

16 "Collaboration: transforming the way business works," a report published by the Economist Intelligence Unit, 2007

17 "National study finds electronics significantly reduce energy use, cut greenhouse-gas emissions," a press release published by the Consumer Electronics Association, September 19, 2007

18 "Fostering Intercompany Collaboration," a commissioned study conducted by Forrester Consulting on behalf of Cisco, October 2010

19 Morten T. Hansen, *Collaboration: How leaders avoid the traps, create unity, and reap big results,* Harvard Business Press, 2009

20 "Meetings Around the World II: Charting the Course of Advanced Collaboration," a study conducted by Frost & Sullivan and sponsored by Cisco and Verizon, 2009

21 "Meetings Around the World II: Charting the Course of Advanced Collaboration," a study conducted by Frost & Sullivan and sponsored by Cisco and Verizon, 2009

22 "Meetings Around the World II: Charting the Course of Advanced Collaboration," a study conducted by Frost & Sullivan and sponsored by Cisco and Verizon, 2009

23 "Return on Collaboration," a report published by Salire Partners, 2010

24 "Return on Collaboration," a report published by Salire Partners, 2010

25 Lowell L. Bryan and Claudia Joyce, "The 21-century organization," *The McKinsey Quarterly,* August 2005

26 "Meetings Around the World II: Charting the Course of Advanced Collaboration," a study conducted by Frost & Sullivan and sponsored by Cisco and Verizon, 2009

27 "Meetings Around the World II: Charting the Course of Advanced Collaboration," a study conducted by Frost & Sullivan and sponsored by Cisco and Verizon, 2009

28 "Unified Communications: Unleashing Transformation, Efficiency, Collaboration, and Compliance," a report published by the Aberdeen Group, March 2010

29 Thomas W. Malone, original interview

30 Thomas W. Malone, *The Future of Work: How the new order of business will shape your organization, your management style, and your life,* Harvard Business Press, 2004

INDEX

V

W

ABOUT THE AUTHORS

As the vice president of corporate positioning, **Ron Ricci** has spent the last decade helping Cisco develop and nurture a culture of sharing and collaborative processes. In addition, he has spent countless hours with hundreds of different organizations discussing the impact of collaboration. He is also the co-author of the business best-seller *Momentum: How Companies Become Unstoppable Market Forces* (Harvard Business Press, 2002).

Carl Wiese is vice president of Cisco's collaboration sales—a multi-billion dollar global business. He has presented on the importance of collaboration to business audiences in dozens of countries, including Australia, China, Dubai, India, Mexico and all across Europe and the United States. With more than 25 years of sales, marketing, services and product-management experience with Cisco, Apple, Lucent, Avaya and Texas Instruments, Wiese has spent his entire career working with companies worldwide to advance their business goals with technology.

At the authors' request, all proceeds from the sale of this book will be shared equally by the Bill Wilson Center (www.billwilsoncenter.org) and the Stanford Cancer Institute (http://cancer.stanford.edu).